I0180987

A-Z

OF WELLBEING
FOR CHILDREN

Lots of ways to look after
your mental health

Ruth Rice and Debbie Green
Illustrated by Debbie Green

Authentic

Copyright © 2025 Ruth Rice and Debbie Green

First published 2025 by Authentic Media Limited,
PO Box 6326, Bletchley, Milton Keynes, MK1 9GG.
authenticmedia.co.uk

The right of Ruth Rice and Debbie Green to be identified as the Authors of this Work has
been asserted in accordance with the
Copyright, Designs and Patents Act 1988.

All rights reserved.
No part of this publication may be reproduced, stored
in a retrieval system, or transmitted in any form or by any means,
electronic, mechanical, photocopying, recording or otherwise, without
the prior permission of the publisher or a licence permitting restricted
copying. In the UK such licences are issued by the Copyright Licensing
Agency, 5th Floor, Shackleton House, 4 Battle Bridge Lane, London SE1 2HX.

British Library Cataloguing in Publication Data
A catalogue record for this book is available from the British Library.
ISBN: 978-1- 78893-397-1
978-1-78893-398-8 (e-book)

Scripture taken from the International Children's Bible® (Anglicised Edition)
© 1991, 2005 by Thomas Nelson, Inc. All rights reserved.

Scripture quotations marked NKJV are taken from the New King James Version®.
Copyright © 1982 by Thomas Nelson. Used by permission. All rights reserved.

Scripture quotations marked NLT are taken from the Holy Bible, New Living Translation,
copyright ©1996, 2004, 2015 by Tyndale House Foundation. Used by permission of Tyndale
House Publishers, Carol Stream, Illinois 60188. All rights reserved.

Scripture quotations marked NIV are taken from
The Holy Bible, New International Version Anglicised
Copyright © 1979, 1984, 2011 Biblica
Used by permission of Hodder & Stoughton Ltd, an Hachette UK company.
All rights reserved.
'NIV' is a registered trademark of Biblica
UK trademark number 1448790.

Cover design by Bekah Grace

Contents

Welcome to the Wellbeing Adventure

Here are some words and thoughts to help you with your wellbeing.

They are words that were very important to me when I wasn't feeling great with my mental health. This A–Z of simple things to do and think about helped me work out how to look after myself better.

I hope they are helpful to you.

Looking after our wellbeing inside and out is really important.

You will probably have your own ideas about how to live with more wellbeing.

You could write your own alphabet when you've had a look at ours.

I wrote this with my sister Debbie. So you will hear both our voices.

I will invite you to explore the Five Ways to Wellbeing which are Connecting, Learning, Getting Active, Taking Notice and Giving. Debbie gets the Learning section where she retells a Jesus story as we think he is the very best teacher when it comes to wellbeing.

Deb has also created some great pictures that you can colour in if you like.

Maybe you could look at one a day or one a week. You could go on this adventure on your own or with a friend, or with someone who cares for you.

There are stories to read, ideas to try, things to do and prayers to pray.

Remember it is OK not to be OK.

And it is also OK to be OK.

Be you!

That is who God made you to be.

Enjoy the Wellbeing adventure!

Ruth and Debbie x

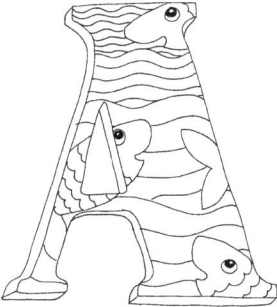

is for Acceptance

CONNECT

What is the best present you have ever had?

When I was a little girl, the best present I ever had was a toy shop that my dad made for me. It had 'Ruth's Store' painted on the front. He had made it just the right size for me and saved lots of sweet wrappers and little boxes to put on the shelves. I can still remember (even though I am very, very old now) running into the front room on Christmas morning when I was 7 years old and seeing that amazing shop and knowing it had been made just for me. I loved it. I straight away ran and thanked Mum and Dad and I *accepted* the gift. It would have been a very different story if I had said that I didn't want it, or that I didn't deserve it and had decided not to accept the present.

Can you imagine how we would all have felt that day?

A gift is made it be accepted.

As we start this journey of wellbeing the first word I really like is *accepted*, not just because it makes me think of lots of goodies I have accepted in the past but because it reminds me that I am accepted by God, that God sees me, made me, loves me and also accepts me like a gift each day, with great delight and love.

I am slowly getting better at accepting myself and being happy to be me, not someone else. I am beginning to understand I am made on purpose like I am right now by a God who really loves and accepts me.

To be accepted and to accept yourself and others is really important for a sense of wellbeing.

LEARN

Peter is accepted LUKE 5:1-11

When someone chooses you do you feel your cheeks lift, your ribcage stretch, your eyebrows arch? Maybe that's just me. I love to be liked. Here's a story about Peter the disciple knowing the joy of being chosen after a particularly difficult night.

Peter is washing his fishing nets, which he isn't very happy about because they are nets that haven't even caught any fish. Jesus is teaching the crowds, which he is really happy about because everyone needs to hear about God's love. Jesus is standing at the very edge of the shore, his sandals are damp as the listening crowds get bigger and the standing space gets smaller. Jesus is happy to accept damp sandals because

they are just sandals, and people are more important, but he asks Peter for help anyway.

'Please can I use your fishing boat as a stage?'

Peter feels his cheeks lift; after such a disappointing night of fishing it's lovely to be picked by Jesus.

Everyone loves hearing what Jesus has to say. Peter hopes he never stops.

Jesus stops.

He turns to Peter.

'Please can we use your boat to go fishing?'

Peter feels his eyebrows dip. Fishing? In the daytime? Fishing? Now, after a long night of proving there aren't any fish around. Fishing? 'If you say so Jesus, let's go fishing.'

Peter is pulling his fishing nets, which he is very happy about and also a bit shocked, as they are completely full and starting to break. Peter is calling his friends to help, which they are very happy about because who wants to miss out on a Jesus miracle?

Peter feels his cheeks sucking in – Jesus can do anything! Does he also know everything? Peter feels his ribs cave a bit – this amazing man shouldn't be in his boat, he's too good.

'Go away from me, Lord; I am a sinful man!' (vv. 8–9).

On his knees among piles of fish, Peter feels ashamed.

'Peter, don't be afraid. I have chosen you to come fishing for people with me.'

Peter feels his cheeks lift, his ribcage stretch and his eyebrows arch. Peter has been chosen by Jesus, accepted just the way he is.

GET ACTIVE

Find a mirror and take a few minutes to have a good look at your face. Lift your eyebrows up really high so you look surprised. Twitch your nose like a rabbit. See how far to one side you can move your mouth. Puff out your cheeks, then suck them in. Open your eyes wide and give a big smile. Do you feel very silly? Good. God loves your face – actually not just your face, he loves every bit of you. He accepts you just the way you are. Some people are never happy about their faces. Have you noticed that? As you stare at your own reflection remember God always sees you. Have you ever seen a parent looking lovingly at the face of their newborn baby? Well God looks lovingly at your face.

You are his creation and he thinks you are great.

How about drawing or painting a self-portrait?

TAKE NOTICE

One of the ways I feel really accepted by God is something I do every day and you might like to try.

When I get up, I make myself a drink in my favourite cup (I have a few favourites so I take a moment to pick which one I want that day). I think of that cup as being like my life. Sometimes it is full, sometimes empty. The cup has been made on purpose and every cup I have is different to all the others. I have chosen them all for different reasons just like we are all made and loved by God.

I then make a drink and find a cosy place to sit and hold the cup in both hands. This reminds me that my life is held in God's hands. God is well-being. The Hebrew word for wellbeing is *shalom*. It is a sort of wholeness that holds me steady even on days when I'm not feeling great. Wellbeing is not a feeling for me, it is a fact. God is wellbeing and my life is held by him always.

I drink my drink slowly and then sit quietly and meditate on a verse from a psalm or a good thought about God.

It makes me feel really accepted. You might not want to do this with a cup, you might think of something else that is precious to you to hold and be still for a moment each day.

GIVE

A question to chat about

What is the best gift you ever accepted?

An idea to try

Can you think of someone who might need to feel more accepted?

Maybe send them a little message or gift. Ask an adult first, please.

A blessing of acceptance

You are accepted
I am too
God loves your face
He made you, you
Thank you, God
That I am me
Your love is enough
It sets me free

B is for Breath

CONNECT

A few years ago, I got poorly. I was a teacher at the time and loved my job. I loved every minute of helping other people learn. But I wasn't good at learning to pace myself and it all got a bit much.

I don't know if you have ever had a time like that when, even though everything is OK, it doesn't feel OK. When I got unwell one of the first things I noticed was that my breathing changed. I wasn't taking deep breaths any more. I was thinking too much and breathing too quickly. The quicker I breathed the more I felt in a bit of a panic.

One of the great things I learnt to do when I was getting better was how to breathe more healthily. Slowly and steadily.

I love to remember that each breath is a gift from God. He breathed life into us and the Bible talks about the Holy Spirit being like wind or breath. I think that helps me when it all gets a bit much.

God himself is breathing life into me. I like that.

LEARN

A breath of fresh air MATTHEW 3:1-17

Take a big breath in, hold your breath and count to three, then let it go with a big 'Baadaah!'

Do you like swimming under water? If you do, you'll know what it's like when your head pops out above the pool and you can fill your lungs with a big satisfying gulp of air. This story is about Jesus going underwater; it starts with some fun facts about his cousin John.

John was an interesting man. He lived in Jesus' time and was a bit of a celebrity. Weirdly, people didn't rush out to see him because he told them lovely stories. They didn't go because he had a nice comfy stadium to sit in and listen. They didn't go to get fashion tips from a snappy dresser. They didn't go for cookery tips. John ate locusts, yes insects, with honey. He wore camel hair, although to be fair he dressed it up a little with a belt. John hung out in the desert, by the river Jordan. And his message for the crowds that came to see him was, 'Say sorry to God. Get ready because he's about to do something awesome.'

How refreshing! John wasn't at all like other people. What a breath of fresh air.

Dipping under the water as a symbol of new life is called baptism and John persuaded people that they needed to get wet, in front of their friends and families to let everyone know they wanted to have a clean start with God.

When Jesus arrived and asked John to baptise him, John was bemused.

'I think it would be more appropriate Jesus if you baptised me! You don't need a new start, you are perfect!'

But Jesus insisted. And the moment that Jesus broke through the surface of the water with all the people watching was unlike anything seen before. Much more than, 'Baadaah! I can breathe!', the Bible says 'heaven opened' (v. 16)!

Wow, breathing the same air as God! Hearing through the atmosphere the very words God speaks. God doesn't open heaven's doors very often; there are few occasions when we get to audibly hear him, so it must have been really important.

God speaks: 'This is my Son and I love him. I am very pleased with him' (v. 17).

And just as God's voice breaks through, so the Spirit of God can't be contained and glides majestically out through the opening between heaven and earth, like a dove, resting on Jesus.

Breathe in the scene, imagine standing on the shore and longing for this moment to last forever – God, Jesus and the Holy Spirit present in your atmosphere.

GET ACTIVE

Get hold of a balloon, or if you don't like balloons get some bubbles, and have a go at blowing as much air into the balloon or through the bubble mixture as you can. What is it like for you blowing out lots of air? Some people have to be careful if they have breathing problems. If that is you, please take extra care.

It is amazing what our breath can do though when it is something we can't even see.

After blowing up balloons (maybe make a balloon animal) or blowing bubbles (you can make your own bubble mix using washing up liquid), take some time to sit down or lie down and just breathe normally.

You can do some great art work blowing through a straw onto some blobs of paint on paper.

TAKE NOTICE

Find somewhere quiet to sit that is really comfy, or lie down and close your eyes. Breathe in through your nose and out through your mouth nice and steadily. Don't think about it too hard. Try to think about *only* the breaths going in and out. Make sure they are slow and steady. Put your hands on your chest as you breathe and feel the air going in and out.

Say a thank you prayer with each breath.

Did you know the Hebrew name for God sounds like breathing in and out? Yahweh. God is in every breath.

GIVE

A question to chat about

Can you think of a time when you have been really aware of your breathing? Why?

An idea to try

Have a go at some of the breathing exercises with a few friends.

A blessing for your breaths

*Your love is
in every breath I take
When I'm asleep
and when I'm awake
Breathe in
Breathe out
and then repeat
God fills me up
from my head to my feet*

C

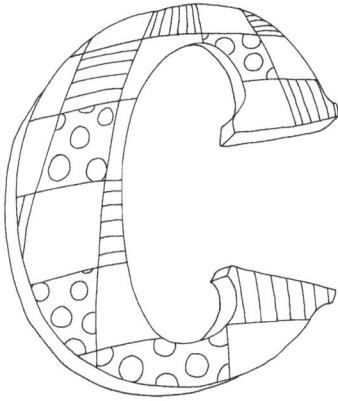

is for Compassion

CONNECT

Have you ever had a time when you felt really silly? A couple of weeks ago I wasn't watching where I was going and I tripped over and I flew! I say I flew because it sounds better than just falling over. I was in a big car park and dashing across to see my son and his family and suddenly found myself flying through the air, landing with a thud on my right knee. It was very painful but I felt so silly too: a grown woman lying in a puddle, not able to get up. But do you know what? No one laughed at me and loads of people came over to see if I was OK. Someone brought me some ice, another ran to get my son and a third person sat down next to me on the ground. They were all showing *compassion*. The word can mean to suffer with someone, to share their difficult moment.

I was very grateful for those strangers in the car park and I am also very grateful for friends and family who show compassion to me all the time. I am even learning to show myself a bit of compassion too. This part of the book might help us get a bit more compassionate.

God is so compassionate to us. He even came as a human to be with us rather than just loving us from a distance.

LEARN

Jesus, the man of compassion MARK 5:21-43

How many different emotions can you think of? Have you ever had a day when you felt like you'd had all of them? Here is a story of a man who felt extremely sad, and he went to Jesus for help.

Poor Jairus. He was used to people coming into the synagogue with their troubles. But this week he was more troubled than any of them. His precious daughter was so very sick. He felt hopeless. An idea raced through his mind – Jesus. Jesus was healing people. Jesus was his only hope.

There was a plethora of people pressing around the healer. Everyone trying to get closer, wanting him to meet their need. Jairus took a deep breath and battled his way to the front of the crowds. Normally a dignified man, Jairus felt too desperate to care about his reputation. He launched himself onto the ground at Jesus' feet. 'My little daughter is dying. Please come and put your hands on her. Then she will be healed and will live' (v. 23).

Jairus led the way, feeling for the first time in weeks that there was hope. He almost smiled. He had Jesus with him, Jesus was following him. He glanced back only to see that Jesus had stopped. Why did Jesus have to have compassion on other people? Couldn't he just focus on his daughter and forget the others?

As Jesus dealt with the very sick woman who had touched him and been healed, Jairus felt his hope draining. His daughter didn't have long. Didn't Jesus realise that? His hope was replaced with a twinge of anger. He'd asked first. Come on Jesus, time is ticking.

Just as Jairus felt it couldn't get worse, he saw his friend in the distance. He could see from his face that the news was bad. His worst fears had come true. His daughter was dead, and they were too late. Jairus collapsed in complete despair. Jesus was there crouching on the ground, face to face, 'Don't be afraid; only believe' (v. 36).

Believe what? It's too late, she's dead. Yet in spite of the impossibility, the look in Jesus' eyes gave Jairus a spark of hope. Jairus in his grief was vaguely aware of the crowds disappearing. Jesus chose three special friends and walked on with Jairus to his home. The house was noisy. Friends and neighbours had turned up to cry and console his broken wife in her grief.

Again he was aware of the crowds dispersing, Jesus sending people away and giving Jairus the space he really craved. He heard Jesus mention sleep. Did he mean his daughter was asleep? No, she was dead, that much was clear.

Jairus watched as Jesus, with tears in his eyes, sat on the edge of his daughter's bed. He picked up her frail, lifeless hand and spoke. 'Little girl, I tell you to stand up!' (v. 41).

Her eyes opened, she sat up and even got straight out of bed. A sudden rush of absolute astonishment and overwhelming gratitude filled Jairus's heart. He looked at Jesus, too emotional to speak. Jesus, the man of compassion, knew his thoughts and emotions. It was enough.

GET ACTIVE

If you want to be someone who is compassionate it can be a good skill to be able to tell what people might be feeling. To do that it helps to know what your own feelings are. I used to be someone who only knew my happy feelings and thought all the other feelings needed fixing. Now I try to accept all my feelings and at least be able to tell if I am sad, angry, worried, happy or hungry. This little activity helps me and I do it most weeks.

I draw a circle and split it into four. In each of the four spaces I write or draw how I am feeling at that moment. I don't think about it too much. I just try to notice it.

You can see then that we are never feeling just one thing. It is usually a mix. I think of it like a hot drink with coffee, milk, water and maybe chocolate sprinkles. It needs all the ingredients.

Maybe a pizza works better for this. A pizza can have a mix of toppings and still be delicious. Maybe there is even a topping you don't like much and other toppings you really like.

Our feelings are what they are. We don't need to judge them. They will change all the time.

How about making a pizza and putting different toppings in different spaces on the pizza whilst thinking about different feelings?

TAKE NOTICE

Spend some time with a friend just listening to them and being with them, rather than doing all the talking or trying to fix them if they are

not OK. Often just being there is enough. You could invite them to do the 'draw a circle' thing with you. Say a quiet prayer for them so that they will know God's love and compassion.

GIVE

A question to chat about

Can you think of a time someone showed you compassion or you showed compassion to someone else? How did it feel?

An idea to try

Ask God if there is someone who needs a compassionate friend today, and if someone comes to mind maybe make them a gift or a card or simply ask them if they are OK today.

A blessing of compassion

May you feel
more compassion
from the God who is love
He's beside
Walking with you
God, here below
Not just up above

D is for Dwell

CONNECT

Do you have a special spot you like to sit in in your house? I always sit in the same place when I'm watching TV. I'm not sure why. I just do. It is my spot. I suppose it makes me feel at home. I also have a chair I like to sit in each morning when I pray, meditate and spend time with God.

I really like it when I visit somewhere that feels like home. There are friends and family I visit where I know I can make myself a drink, curl up on the sofa, choose the programme we are watching and help set the table. These are places where you can make yourself at home. Do you have places like that?

God invites us to make ourselves at home in him. I like to think of that as having such a close relationship with God that I can feel like I am curling up with him and know I am welcome. He also says he wants to make himself at home in our lives. Is God welcome in all your thoughts and actions?

Another word for making yourself at home is 'dwelling'. I sometimes refer to this sense of feeling loved, welcome and cosy in God as 'dwellbeing'.

Choosing to dwell with Jesus LUKE 10:38-42

Being busy can be fun, it's usually useful and makes us feel needed. Being still involves some self-discipline. Martha in this story is extremely busy, but her sister Mary chooses to sit still. This causes a problem.

Martha's in a flap. He's not just any guest – he's their favourite guest. And meals don't cook themselves. It's important to make things look orderly when you have visitors. It crosses Martha's mind that maybe she wants her visitors to see that she's a bit of a martyr, always putting in the extra effort. Whilst she picks up clothes and rattles pans, she imagines distant conversations focused on her. 'Oh, Martha is such a selfless, giving person. Nothing is too much trouble. Did you see her bustling around making things just right for us? What a shame her sister can't be more like her.'

Mary, she's just sitting there. Martha knocks a couple of pans together to make the point that she's busy, hoping to catch Mary's eye. Nope. Mary doesn't blink, her gaze fixed on Jesus. Brilliant. Thanks, Mary, for all the help. Bristling with jealousy, Martha makes a bold decision. 'Jesus, don't you care that my sister has left me to do all the work? Tell her to help me!' (v. 40).

Jesus pauses his teaching to the disciples and Mary and looks at Martha, who is sweating and a bit breathless.

'Martha, Martha,' Jesus says, 'You are getting worried and upset about too many things. Only one thing is important. Mary has chosen the right thing, and it will never be taken away from her' (v. 42).

What is it that Mary has chosen?

Everything Jesus says makes Mary's ears tingle. These words don't just make sense, they bring inspiration, hope, joy, freedom, life. Even the fact that Martha is clattering about disrespectfully can't distract Mary now. She daren't miss a syllable. To have Jesus in their home is such an honour, to have him teach in her home is amazing, but to be included is ridiculous! Where else would Mary ever be allowed to sit and learn at a rabbi's feet? Only Jesus shows this kind of fairness. Only Jesus speaks the words that make her want to live for the glory of God. In her mind, Mary repeats some of his phrases, determined to remember as much as possible. She could sit here forever, dwelling in the presence of the greatest teacher, kindest rabbi, most wonderful example to everyone, even her. If only Martha would stop crashing about and join in. It's a divine moment and sadly her sister has completely missed it.

GET ACTIVE

This time it is the opposite of getting active that we need to have a go at. I wonder how long you can stay still for? Get a timer and see if you can stay completely still for a whole minute. If you can . . . well done. Try 2 minutes. What did it feel like being a statue? If you haven't got a timer, you could make one out of two bottles with some sand in them, taped together at the opening. More sand equals longer time. A smaller hole for the sand to run through also changes the amount of time. Play with it until you get a 1-minute timer.

Maybe play a game of musical statues. You can even play this by yourself. It is better with friends, but if it is just you, try dancing wildly to your favourite music, then suddenly stopping the music for a whole minute and seeing how still you can stand before starting it again.

TAKE NOTICE

Every morning, I do the same prayer in the same spot. I use a few verses from Psalm 103 to help me pray (see the prayers at the end of the book). It helps to calm me down and gets me ready for the day.

If you want to try this, pick a chair or a cosy spot and put the things that help you to pray nearby. I have a notebook, a pen, a Bible and a little battery-operated candle. I also have a special cup.

As I pray and sit still in my spot I feel like I can put all my weight on God just like I am putting all my weight on the chair. It helps me relax and be at home, or dwell in God.

GIVE

A question to chat about

Where do you feel most at home and why?

An idea to try

Invite some friends or family to be at home with you. Make some snacks, play some games, watch a movie. Chat about what home means to people. You are being a good host when you make people feel at home. God is a great host and always invites us to be at home in his presence.

A blessing for dwellbeing

*Dwell in me, God
as I choose to dwell in you
Help me remember
you dwell in me too*

*So make yourself at home
in my heart and in my head
in every moment of this day
until I get back into bed*

E is for Empty

 **CONNECT**

In my alphabet of wellbeing this word might seem a bit of a strange one to choose. How can being empty be good for you? Surely emptiness is a bad thing?

Sometimes I do feel quite empty inside. Have you ever felt like that? I can remember feeling very down one day when I was unwell and the day felt long and empty. Often my days are very full and my mind is even fuller of thoughts and plans. Strangely it was at a time in my life when I felt a bit empty that I really connected with God. I suppose I had some space and some time to really listen and when I did hear God speaking to me (it wasn't like a big booming voice, more like an idea in my own head, like a whisper) I think this is what I heard:

> Ruth, I love you. I could not love you any more and will never love you any less than I do right now.

What was amazing was that I heard this when I didn't feel like I was much use. I felt empty. I wasn't doing anything helpful to make God pleased with me.

My emptiness gave some space for God to fill me up.

LEARN

Full of questions MATTHEW 19:16-23

God loves us to come to him with empty hands. Here's a story of a young man who didn't just have full hands because he was very rich, but he had filled his life with his own plan of trying to do good works to earn a place in God's kingdom.

Here is a young man. He has a question for Jesus. It won't be difficult to find him, he just needs to follow the crowds.

He finds Jesus surrounded by children. These children bring nothing to Jesus, their hands are empty. He thinks about how he might contribute a small donation to Jesus' little group of disciples. At last Jesus looks up and our young man takes the opportunity, 'Teacher, what good thing must I do to have life forever?' (v. 16).

So relieved to have asked his question, he almost forgets to listen to the answer. This question has been keeping him awake at night. It niggles at him, even though he's been a good person all his life. He just needs a bit of clarification and this man Jesus seems to have a hotline to God. He's pretty sure he's ticked the right boxes but his brain won't switch off. He just wants to sleep peacefully again. He realises Jesus is talking about the commandments.

'I have obeyed all these things. What else do I need to do?' says the man (v. 20).

As soon as he'd asked the second question, he regretted it. Why ask about more? Perhaps he is showing off.

'If you want to be perfect, then go and sell all the things you own. Give the money to the poor. If you do this, you will have treasure in heaven. Then come follow me!' Jesus said (v. 21).

Sell everything! No, that can't be right! Empty out his bank account, his pockets? It's just impractical. Jesus has missed the point. He just wanted to do a good thing and know that he'd done enough. Giving up what he has isn't an option. Being good was his plan, so good that God would allow him to be part of his kingdom. Perhaps there were other ways to get to sleep. Perhaps someone else had a better answer.

The young man turns his back on Jesus, and as he walks away, he feels empty inside.

GET ACTIVE

Here is an activity for days when you feel like your head is full of worries.

Take a cup. You can use your special cup. Look at how empty it is. Now cut up lots of bits of paper or gather lots of small stones. Write on each piece of paper or each stone something that is worrying you.

Place each one into the cup carefully until the cup is full up.

Now simply turn the cup upside down and say a short prayer giving all those worries to God for him to sort out.

Take your empty cup and hold it in your hands. Know that you are held and loved.

Now wash out the cup and fill it up with your favourite drink and take a moment to enjoy it.

(Don't forget to go back and clear up all the paper or stones later, by the way!)

TAKE NOTICE

Sit quietly in your thinking chair or prayer spot. Hold out your hands, palms facing up and imagine all the things that are worrying you held in your hands. Know that God can see and can hold those things. When you are ready turn your hands over palms facing down and picture handing all those things that worry you over to God.

GIVE

A question to chat about

What does the word 'empty' make you think about? Is it a good or a bad thing?

An idea to try

It can be a good idea to pick up a hobby that you are good at and get stuck in to it if you are feeling a bit empty. You could try asking a friend for help if you can't think of anything to do.

A blessing of emptiness

*May you be empty enough
to receive the gift God brings today
And may you get filled with his love
as you slow down, show up and pray*

F is for Family

CONNECT

The idea of family can be tricky for some people, can't it?

Not all families are the same. I really like mine. Maybe you can tell because I am writing this book with my sister, Debbie. She has written all the Jesus stories and done all the amazing pictures in this book. We have another sister too. We all get on and really love each other. Well, we do now. When we were younger, we used to fight and fall out. Sometimes we would even try to hurt each other's feelings. I can't believe we used to do that. We are all very old now and I'm very glad I have family that love me and accept me just as I am.

But family doesn't have to be just the people who you called family when you were born. That would be really hard for people who don't have any family or for whom their family is difficult.

The Bible tells about us becoming family to each other and God being our Father. It also says that God himself is three persons in one, Father, Son and Spirit. He is three in one. We are told to love each other and treat each other like brothers and sisters.

Learning to be family can be hard but it can also be good for our wellbeing.

My job running the charity 'Renew Wellbeing' is to help churches be more like families and open up cafés where people can come and belong and look after their wellbeing. Lots of people find this helps if they are lonely. One of my favourite verses in the psalms says, 'God sets the lonely in families' (Ps. 68:6, NIV).

 **LEARN**

Four friends feeling ambitious MARK 2:1-12

Do you have friends you can share everything with? In this story a paralysed man has four good friends. They help him with all the things he can't do for himself and they know what he's really like. They've seen him when he's horribly grumpy. They are like family to him.

Today I am hoping my four friends come to visit. I can't go to visit them, I can't move. I just wait, lying on my bed hoping for something to brighten my day.

Here they are: 'Come on, Jesus is in Capernaum, let's go and get you healed!'

Well, that's a new idea. My four friends are feeling ambitious today. As they pick up my bed, one in each corner, I'm grinning, but trying not to let myself imagine being able to walk, it's too exciting.

'I knew it,' I grumbled, seeing crowds pressing around the house where Jesus is. It's been a long walk, for them, not me; and a heavy burden, for them, not me. 'We can't possibly reach Jesus,' I mumble, almost feeling cross that they got my hopes up.

One of my four friends looks me in the eye.

'Today is the day. Ready to do something audaciously daring?' I don't have a chance to answer. My four friends are huddled in a scheming group, all I can hear is the occasional, 'What!' 'Are you sure that will work?'

Wishing I could jump off my bed and join them, I'm feeling less and less daring.

Suddenly we're off. They've picked up my bed again and raced round to the back of the house. They seem to be heading to the steps that take you up to the flat roof. They see my face.

'Don't worry, it's a brilliant plan and we will keep you safe.'

It must have been so tiring to get me up to the roof without me slipping off the bed. But they don't seem tired – my friends are peeling back layers of plaster from the roof! They are making a hole. We don't even know whose house it is, and yet, for my sake they are prepared to get into trouble.

'I can see Jesus,' shouts one friend. 'Dig more in this direction, let's deliver him straight to the healer.'

With ropes tied securely to the corners of my bed and a massive hole in the roof, my four daring, loving, reckless, generous friends lower me slowly and carefully over the heads of the dumbstruck crowd. I can hear grumbling below me as people shove each other to get out of the way. But I can only see above me – four faces, teeth clenched, straining with the weight of me and my bed, and four pairs of eyes, sparkling with excitement, looking straight into mine causing my own eyes to well up with grateful tears.

Jesus, just like my friends, knows all about me. He knows that my biggest worries are about my grumpiness, my selfishness, my sin. So Jesus deals with it all. He heals my heart from all my bad choices and he heals my legs so I can run outside, find my four friends and squeeze them and thank them, cry happy tears with them and begin to show them how much they mean to me.

GET ACTIVE

Can you name a few people that are like family to you? It might be your friends.

Maybe you could try including someone in your group who is feeling left out or who looks lonely.

It can be hard to include other people when we are having fun with the people we know well, but have a look round next time you are enjoying a game or a chat with friends and give it a try. Imagine how you would feel if you were the one left out.

Have you ever made a paper chain of people? You can do it by cutting out and sticking together lots of little people from card or paper. Or you can be clever and fold a strip of paper back and forth and then only have to cut out one person and you end up with a whole chain of people. You may need to try this several times but it is a great way to use up scrap paper and you might come up with a whole new way of making chains of people. Go on, give it a try. Write the name of someone to pray for on each person in the chain.

TAKE NOTICE

When you are praying for your family or group of friends it can help to use your fingers so you don't forget anyone. You could think of each person in your family as you look at each finger.

I also do a strange thing where I ask God to show me an animal that reminds me of members of my family, and whenever I see that animal I

remember to pray for the family member and say a blessing. It sounds odd but let me explain.

One of my children makes me think of a swan, another of a robin and the third of a bird of prey. I'm not sure why. They just do. So when I am out for a walk or watching TV and any of these birds pop up, I always stop and pray for that member of my family.

That might be too odd for you but do whatever helps you pray every day for those you love.

GIVE

A question to chat about

What does the word 'family' make you think of?

An idea to try

Maybe you could join a group that all do the same sport or hobby, if you aren't part of one already. It can be good to belong. Maybe you could start a group.

A blessing for family

Father, who holds us
Son, who enfolds us
Spirit, who gives love a voice
Teach us to love
Like you first loved us
To be deep-hearted family
Not as duty but choice[1]

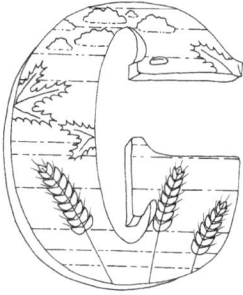

G is for Growth

CONNECT

I like trying to do gardening. I love plants and flowers, and thought if I popped a few bulbs and seeds in the ground and kept an eye on them I could have a wonderful tidy space, just like my neighbour's garden.

The seeds looked good, the plants I bought were lovely too. So, I was a bit disappointed when after digging little holes and popping the seeds in, I saw very little for my effort. Most didn't grow at all. The things that did grow I later discovered were weeds.

You see, the trouble was I hadn't prepared the soil at all. I didn't even dig very deep holes. The place I decided to grow my flowers had been part of a stream that the last owners had dug, and what I hadn't realised was that they had removed all the soil and replaced it with sand, stones, a carpet and a pond liner so that a little stream could flow. The stream had dried up and a layer of shallow soil had formed over the place it had

been. Because I didn't dig deeply enough, I didn't know any of this. All my plants, bulbs and seeds just died as they had nowhere for the roots to go, and no moisture.

This year I took a bit longer and dug a lot deeper. It took ages and several bags of compost but I now do have green things growing, and even though I would not say I am a gardener, I am learning that plants need care for their roots that you can't see, not just the stem and flowers that you can see.

I am also understanding that my life is like a plant and that I need to take care of my thoughts and emotions that no one but God can see, not just my actions and words that everyone else gets to see and hear.

The Bible talks about our roots needing to go down deep into God's love.

LEARN

Graham, Gwen, Gladys and Greg MATTHEW 13:1-23

Did you know the Bible compares us to soil? Yes, strange hey? Jesus tells a story about a man sowing seed onto four types of soil. He wanted his disciples to think about the different reactions people had when they heard the good news of God's love.

A story about growth, or lack of it. Let's have a look at the four reactions to God's seed of hope.

Reaction one: A seed that falls on the path. We all know seeds need roots to grow and this one has no chance. Let's name this reaction Graham. Graham doesn't even listen to the good news. He isn't into religion. He's happy enough to believe life happens to you and then that's it. So that's it. The seed remains a seed. Until some birds come. Look out, Graham!

Reaction two: A seed that falls on rocky places. There's a bit of soil between the rocks, not a lot. But let's call this reaction Gwen. Gwen hears that God loves her and she can come to Jesus and be rescued. Great news. Gwen puts down some roots and prepares for some healthy growth. Then Gwen starts to find things tricky. Not everyone agrees this is good news and she starts to doubt her choices. She doesn't want to be picked on for choosing to be different. Perhaps it isn't worth it after all. Gwen stops growing. The sun comes out and Gwen's roots haven't found any moisture. She's had enough.

Reaction three: A seed that falls into thorns. The soil is good, it's just that this little seed has to share it with some great big weeds. Let's call this reaction Gladys. Gladys, like Gwen, hears the good news of God's kingdom and accepts this new way of life as a good idea. Who doesn't want forgiveness, eternal life and Jesus with them every day? But then Gladys also loves stuff. She finds the buzz of buying stuff a bit addictive. In fact, Gladys starts to believe that what the world offers seems more fun than what God offers. Eventually she finds that owning things and making money has choked out any thoughts of God and his kingdom. God's kingdom is all about humility, generosity and sacrifice.

Reaction four: A seed that fell onto good soil. Let's call this reaction Greg. Greg gets it. He hears the good news and just like Gwen and Gladys he accepts this good news. He is hungry and thirsty to know more about Jesus and God's kingdom. His roots go deep into God's Word and his growth is reflected in the way he feeds. Greg hears, sees and understands what he is offered. He isn't going to allow troubles to stop him or the world to distract him. Greg is maturing and bearing fruit. He's producing seeds and helping others to grow too.

Let's be like Greg.

🕺 GET ACTIVE

Have you got a garden? If so it's time to get out and pull up a few weeds and maybe plant some seeds. If not, you can grow things in just a bit of soil in a pot on the windowsill, you know. Maybe you could help with someone else's garden. There are rewilding projects in lots of towns too that you can help with. This is a way to help attract wildlife to built-up areas and help our planet to breathe better.

Gardening is also really good, free exercise.

You could try growing some things to eat. Herbs. tomatoes, potatoes and lettuce are all easy to grow.

📝 TAKE NOTICE

Next time you eat a piece of fruit with seeds in. save the seeds and dry them out. Hold one seed in your hand and sit quietly. Look at it for a moment before you plant it, and see if you can grow anything from it. A seed is amazing, as it can be really small but it has all the life needed to produce a plant hidden inside it. It is not until that seed goes into the dark of the ground, hidden away, that it can really start to grow.

As you look after your seed / little plant, know that God looks after you carefully and that he has placed within you all that is needed for you to grow and be completely you.

GIVE

A question to chat about

Have you ever managed to grow anything? What did you learn?

An idea to try

How about designing a garden of your dreams, and then maybe getting together with some friends and seeing if you can plant some of it? Sometimes people will lend you some land if you don't have any yourself. Some schools have gardening groups or might let you start one. Growing things together can be great fun. There are allotment projects you might be able to join in with.

A blessing for growth

Great gardener of my soul and mind
Please come and clear the weeds you find
You are the soil
I am the seed
and your deep love
is all I need

H is for Hope

CONNECT

'Hope' is a funny word, isn't it? I love it, but when I use it in a sentence it sometimes loses its real meaning. I can say that I hope this day turns out alright. When I chat to friends I often say that I hope they will be OK. Or sometimes I even hope someone will buy me some chocolate. What I am saying is a sort of wishful thinking; I am not at all sure and would just really like these things to be true. But when the Bible speaks about hope, it is a much stronger meaning. God gives us hope 'and this hope will never disappoint us' (Rom. 5:5). So that means it's a hope for something that is certain to be true. The hope we have in God's love is sure and something solid to hold onto. When I say I put my hope in God, it means I am not just saying I wish God would love me, it is saying that I *know* and can be sure God loves me.

I think I used to treat God more like a genie in a pot and hope that if I prayed enough, he might show up. Now I am trying each day to practise real hope when I am praying.

Whether I see the answers or not, I know God loves me, wants the best for me and is really there. This hope helps my wellbeing so much.

🧠 LEARN

Drachma in the dust LUKE 15:8-10

How many times have I put my glasses down and within minutes lost them? Know that feeling? Searching the house; trying every windowsill, table top and cushion? This task, of course, is made all the more difficult when you don't have your glasses. Here is a story Jesus told about a lost coin. Let's think about how the coin felt!

It's hopeless. Have you seen this house? If she finds me under here it will be a miracle. Not only is this room too dark, but these floors are made of earth. It's not that they are dusty – they are dust! Then there's the clutter. This lady owns sixty-four clay pots and jars, and these jars are sitting on top of seven small woven rugs. Not to mention the table, the chairs, the cushions and clothes. I don't stand a chance. I'm underneath all of this. She didn't even see me roll away. Didn't notice my absence. One minute I'm with my buddies and the next I'm tumbling across the floor, under the table, around the chairs and pots and end my journey with a sliding stop tucked under a rug. And I'm no longer a shiny silver colour, now the dust has settled on my face – you can't tell me from the dirt around me.

I'm not even sure she will look that hard. I'm just one of ten, she still has the other nine. In one day she could earn enough to replace me. I bet that's what she's decided. I'm not worth the effort.

It's been such a long time. I did see her light a lamp, it gave me a glimmer of hope, but that lamp has moved all over the room and although for a moment it glinted in my direction, it didn't stop. I've noticed the brush and pan have come to help. From here I could see her sweeping under the table, lifting the pots, brushing into corners that I've never seen her brush before. She came towards me at one point, again hope swept my way, but I'm in an awkward place, not easy to spot.

Now this is a new tactic. She's started to the clear the room. One by one she's lifting the pots and jars and putting them outside the house, carefully checking inside each one. She's managed to heave the five chairs out of the door and is standing looking at the table, considering how to begin. She's doing it! I didn't know she had the strength, dragging the large wooden table to the door, and now realising it will never fit through. But that gives her room to lift the rugs. One, two, three – each one lifted carefully, shaken, brushed and rolled up onto the table. Four, five, six – don't give up now, I'm here, I'm here under rug number seven! She's looking very tired. Her face reminds me of the hopelessness I felt three hours ago. The seventh rug is being lifted. She's on her hands and knees. I can see now that her clothes are covered in dust from her long and fruitless search.

Dry, cracked, dirty, hurting hands brush across my dusty face. She's found me. I'm clean and I'm saved. And with all the furniture gone there is room for dancing. Dancing with all the neighbours. Dancing until the sun goes down. She must really care about me. She never gave up hope.

GET ACTIVE

It would be great if everyone could find hope, wouldn't it?

So this activity might help spread a little bit of hope.

Get some nice smooth stones. You can collect some from outside if you have permission and clean them or even buy them from a garden centre.

Write the word 'HOPE' on the stone and decorate it. Start with pencil to get the design, then use acrylic paints or permanent pens.

Make bold colourful designs on the stones. You could even put little encouraging messages or Bible verses on the back.

When the paint or pen is dry, varnish the stone with PVA glue. When they are ready, go and leave them in places where they might be found by strangers or friends. When you are out on a walk next, you could leave your stones on benches or in places where people might find them, and either take them or just enjoy them.

TAKE NOTICE

I really like stone painting, so if you do too, then maybe use some little stones to help you as you pray or to help others to pray. Use fine marker pens to write names on stones of people you are praying for. Have a few other little pebbles with encouraging words about how much God loves you on them. Words like peace, love, joy and hope can be helpful. I like to then choose a stone to hold as I pray, and think about that word and pray for that person.

You could make some prayer stones for other people and write little blessings on them like 'May God give you peace today'.

Have a little pot of prayer stones and keep it near your prayer spot, or pop a prayer stone in your pocket so you can feel it there and know God is with you through the day.

GIVE

A question to chat about

When have you felt hopeful or hopeless?

An idea to try

A friend of mine taught me how to use a big scrap book to help with hope. Collect any pictures, photos, words or stories that fill you with hope and stick them in your hope book. You can do this all in one go using old magazines to make it look colourful, or you can keep this as an ongoing project for many years and just add to it when you see something hopeful.

A blessing for hope

> *May the God of all peace*
> *fill you with hope*
> *that is more than wishes that may come true*
> *But truth and love*
> *and a knowing deep down*
> *that God will always, always love you*

I is for Interests

CONNECT

When I was a teacher I loved my job, but I think I forgot that I wasn't just a teacher, I was a human being and I got a bit busy and forgot to look after myself properly. I am now learning that God made me with lots of things that I can do that make me more me. The Bible talks about us being God's masterpieces (Eph. 2:10, NLT). I love that. He spends time making and forming us and because we are made in his image we also have things we like to create and do.

When I got ill, I had to learn to slow down and do some 'just because' things. These are things that don't always feel like they are a good use of time. But actually, they are things that help us to become a masterpiece.

I like painting stones. I like crochet. I love gardening and making old things into new things by sewing or sticking. I like sanding down wooden things. I like swimming in the sea and reading a good book (not at the same time!). I like walking my dog and playing games with my family. I like a meal with mates or time on my own by the sea.

What do you like to do?

Making time for your interests is a big part of you becoming you.

LEARN

Taking an interest MATTHEW 25:14-30

I believe God gives us all interests. He knows what it is to be creative or productive and he wants us to enjoy that satisfaction too. He trusts us with talents. Here's a story Jesus told about three people who were trusted with something. It's not exactly the way he told it, but the idea is the same.

The boss called Ian, Indigo and Ivy into his room.

'I'm off on a journey and I need each of you to take an interest in these gifts.' He dragged out from under his desk a large wooden treasure chest and opened it carefully.

'Ian, you've worked hard for me in the past. I am going to give you five bags. You might need something on wheels to get it home, it's quite heavy.'

Ian saw his boss lift out one heavy hessian bag; placing it carefully at Ian's feet, he went back for four more and invited Ian to look inside. It was gold! Ian felt so honoured to be trusted with his boss's precious treasure. 'Thank you, sir. You won't be sorry.' His mind immediately turned to all the ideas he had for investing it.

'Indigo, you can probably manage to carry these home. Here are two bags of gold. Enjoy using them and let your imagination run wild.' Indigo smiled, took the bags with some difficulty and nodded to her boss.

Ian could see that Ivy was glancing towards the door. Wasn't she excited?

'Ivy, anything wrong?' asked the boss. She shook her head with such a tiny motion it was more a shiver than a head shake. 'I have something here for you too.'

The boss handed her one bag of gold. She took it slowly and reluctantly, and placed it on the floor by her feet, almost as if she were ashamed of it.

It was many months later that the boss invited his three employees back to his office.

'Ian, how did you get on?'

Ian was beaming. 'Sir, I'd just like to thank you for entrusting me with your gold. There are lots more creative ideas I would love to try, but here is what I managed, sir.' Ian left the room for a moment and returned with a shopping trolley loaded with bags of gold. Ten bags of gold! He'd doubled the boss's gift.

'Well done, Ian, I've got big plans for you. Now Indigo, I see you have something to show me.'

'Yes, sir,' said Indigo. 'I took your two bags of gold and worked hard at letting my imagination run wild. I hope you are pleased. Here are four bags, sir.'

'I'm very pleased, Indigo. I've got big plans for you too. Now, has anyone seen Ivy?'

Ian had spotted her in the corridor when he'd been out to get his trolley full of gold. She peered around the doorframe.

'Ivy, come here and tell me all about your time whilst I was away. Did you enjoy using the gold I gave you?'

Ivy walked into the room holding one dusty hessian bag – the same bag she was given. 'Here you go. I haven't touched it. You can count it, it's the same as what you left me.' She plonked her bag carelessly on the desk and stepped back.

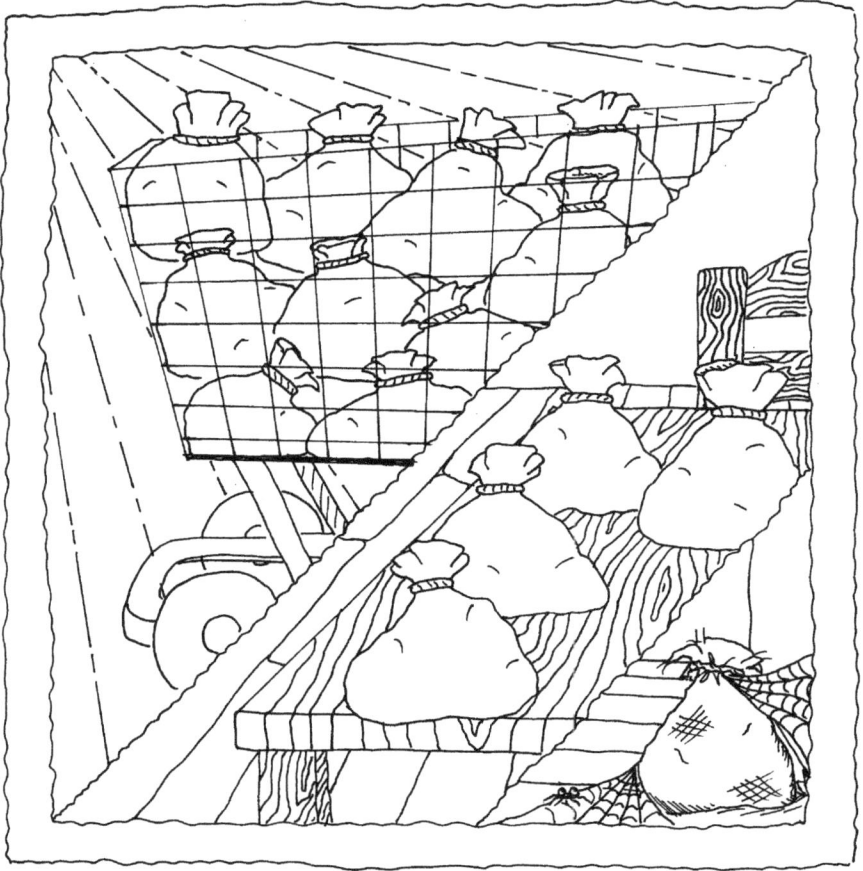

GET ACTIVE

Well, this getting active is easy. Just go and spend some time doing something you love doing. If you can't think of anything, maybe it is time to start a new hobby. Ask your friends to teach you one of their hobbies. Sports, crafty stuff, outdoors, indoors . . . there are loads of things that help our wellbeing. Maybe join a club or learn something new online. Hobbies are sometimes called recreation. Can you see 'creation' in that word? When we do these fun things, I think we are being re-created by God to be more and more the person he made us to be.

TAKE NOTICE

One of the things that is said to be really good for your wellbeing and help you if your thoughts start getting troublesome is to do a repeated action over and over again. For me this is what happens when I do crochet. It is very repetitive. It is also what happens when I meditate on a phrase from the Bible over and over in my head. Try colouring in something slowly, or walking carefully and taking notice of what the ground feels like under your feet with each step. Whatever hobby or activity it is, make some time to really take notice of what you are doing and how it feels. As you do this, know that God is smiling and joining in when you are fully present in the moment.

GIVE

A question to chat about

What hobbies and interests do you love? What new one would you like to try?

An idea to try

In our Renew centres, that the charity I work for sets up, we encourage people to show up and bring a hobby, and maybe bring something extra for someone who hasn't got a hobby. Could you start a little group with some friends where you teach each other things that help your wellbeing? If there is a Renew centre near you, then you could go along with an adult, or ask them if they might start a session for children and youth. There is training for churches who would like to have a go at this and it is *free*.

A blessing for your interests

God, who made all people
and everything we see
Please recreate wellbeing
right here, right now, in me

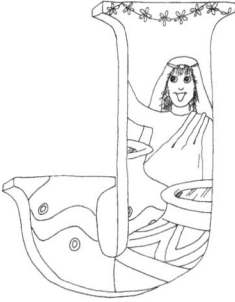

is for Joy

CONNECT

When I was a child, I used to think it was only OK for me to be happy all the time and that if I wasn't happy, I was letting God down. I had learned a verse from the Bible that told me God's joy was my strength (Neh. 8:10, NIV) and so I thought that meant I had to smile and be jolly all the time. I now understand that joy is not the same as happiness. The word 'happiness' comes from a word that is all about our circumstances, and we all know that our circumstances are not jolly all the time. We all have difficult days. So, what does the Bible mean about joy being our strength, then?

I think of joy now as like the bass note in a really good song. You know that you can hear other notes, sometimes happy and sometimes sad, in the main tune. But there can be a bass note, a deeper rhythm, a drumbeat, even, that is always there. This is what joy is like for me. Joy is more than a feeling, it is a fact. God is with me. He loves me so I have a joy that cannot be unsettled, and can exist at the same time as sad things.

Being joyful doesn't mean I have to laugh and be jolly all the time. What a relief.

LEARN

Miracles in the mundane JOHN 2:1-11

Have you ever been doing something really mundane and everyday, and suddenly realised you were feeling joyful? I often catch myself singing when I'm tidying the kitchen, which is strange. Surely I'm not enjoying it? I think we can be content even when we are having to do ordinary things. In this story, Abigail the servant understands that.

Abigail has been serving in the same household for quite a long time. She's known to bring with her an atmosphere of contentment. This attitude wasn't generally found. Many of the servants were jealous of their master's wealth; dissatisfied with their lot and angry that just because they were born into the wrong family, they found themselves slaving away for the benefit of others.

Today is a special day, and Abigail is determined to spread her joy among the other servants. The master's daughter is to be married, and whilst this means much more work for the household servants, it also means a joyful celebration that is expected to last for days.

With a spring in her step, Abigail hangs up decorations, prepares food, sets out tables, and most importantly, helps her master's daughter with her clothes and preparations. Everything is ready, and although Abigail hasn't sat down for most of the day, she knows the effort will pay off. Looking around, the bride and bridegroom sit whispering to each other, while at a table heaving with good things to eat, their parents watch the dancers twirl and swish around the dance floor. Abigail's senses are overwhelmed with the brightly coloured clothing, the warmth of

so many people in one place and the sound of laughter, music and animated conversation. It is then that she sees some of her friends huddled in the corner, heads close together talking, their faces displaying something far from joyous. She goes to offer help.

'John hasn't bought enough wine; it's almost gone. He doesn't know who to ask so late in the evening. The master of the feast will be furious.'

Abigail has an idea. She knows a lady called Mary, a guest at the wedding. She's so wise and caring – she will know what to do.

Mary is consulted and she goes straight to her son. At first Jesus seems reluctant, but his solution surprises everyone.

'Jesus says to fill our six massive jars with water,' says Abigail. 'Let's do it quickly.' Back and forth they run with pots of water, filling the jars to the brim.

'Now take some out and give it to the master of the feast,' Jesus says (v. 8). The servants seem to hesitate. Abigail doesn't. She runs and dips in a cup, handing it to John with a huge grin. John looks into the cup and his face makes Abigail want to shout for joy.

John offers the cup to the master of the feast who takes it to try. 'You have saved the best wine till now,' he says (v. 10). John looks back to the others, pure joy on his face. Only they know how this wine appeared – a miracle that most people will just see as a tasty choice.

Next week they will all go back to their mundane chores. But Abigail's prayer is that John and her friends remember this joyful moment and look for God's miracles in their day-to-day tasks.

GET ACTIVE

It is time to play. Whatever your age reading this book, playtime is a good time. Go outside. Take a look around and spot a few things that make you smile or give you a glowing sense deep down. Think of something you would like to do; maybe run, jump, skip, climb, lie down quietly, spin round and round, kick a ball or look closely at a flower. We are all different, so what you notice and what you do will be different for each person, but see if you can sense some joy and get your whole body to join in.

TAKE NOTICE

On a walk, spot things that make you smile, and make a list of them.

Take pictures or draw things that bring you joy.

Pause over each thing and say thank you to God for that thing or person.

GIVE

A question to chat about

What brings you joy? Is it different from happiness?

An idea to try

See if you can think of something that will bring joy to someone else. Send a gift, pop round to see someone, suggest an activity. Shared joy is the best sort of joy.

A blessing for joy

There is joy
in every detail
of this world that you have made
Lord, help me hear your joy notes
in every place I've worked and played

K is for Kindness

CONNECT

The Bible talks about us putting on kindness. I think we usually all remember to get dressed before we go out each day, don't we? I am trying to think about God's kindness like clothes that I need to put on every day. Being kind means speaking kindly, thinking kindly and doing kind things. We can remember to do this towards other people, but are you kind to yourself?

I remember being asked to write a letter to my younger self, giving her some advice. I wrote all sorts of things about being more grateful and not taking myself too seriously and trying harder. Then forgot all about it. The person who asked us to write the letter sent it to us a year later. Can you imagine getting a letter addressed to you in your own writing when you had forgotten all about it? Spooky!

But when I opened it, I was a bit upset. I had not treated myself kindly. I would never have been so bossy with anyone else. All the words were full of criticism, not encouragement. I didn't keep that letter but I did learn to speak more kindly in my head, to treat myself with kindness like I would someone else.

The Bible says we are to love others as we love ourselves (Matt. 22:39). So, are you being kind to you?

LEARN

A kind stranger LUKE 10:25-37

There are opportunities for kindness all around us. I wonder how often we feel it's not our responsibility? Jesus told a very well-known story; let's hear it from the traveller's point of view.

I was bowled over by that man's kindness. Seriously, I thought my number was up. It's a journey I've done dozens of times before and to be fair, always felt a bit vulnerable. You do hear stories of robbers on that lonely mountain path to Jericho, but you never think it's going to happen to you.

It happened to me, and it was a terrible experience. They not only took my money bag, but also my cloak and some of my clothes, and as if that wasn't enough, they hit and kicked me, too many times to count. Then they left. Left me with mixed feelings. Relieved that they were gone, angry at having been treated with such inhumanity and, most of all, anxious that this was how I would end my days. I was alone, bleeding, unable to get myself onto my feet and it would get dark soon.

You can imagine how relieved I was to hear footsteps in the distance and as the man came closer my heart leapt for joy to see it was a priest. Priests preached about kindness all the time. I know he saw me. You

couldn't miss me, lying at the side of the path. I managed a pitiful, 'Help!' but it just seemed to make him more determined to hurry on. He was scanning the hills around, checking for the robbers. Then he was gone.

Again I lay there alone, reflecting on what I would do if I were him. Would I be kind enough to stop and help? Or would I be wary of the danger, the blood, the awkwardness of helping a stranger? I started to think I might not have stopped either.

Another traveller came near; this time a Levite. Well, these people were known for working in the temple. Surely helping the needy was part of their work? You can't get much more needy than a man at risk of dying on a desolate mountain road. He had that look in his eye: he knew he should help but he hoped someone else would do it. He looked around. There was no one else. And yet, shaking his head and glancing behind him one last time, he disappeared out of sight.

I had decided to give up hope. No one would put themselves out for a stranger.

And then another sound, another traveller. As he came closer, my heart sank. It was a Samaritan. Now, if I were a Samaritan, if I'd always been rejected just because of where I was born, then I know how I'd react. Not that I personally treat Samaritans badly, but then again, I have never objected openly.

But that man was suddenly crouching next to me, muttering some words of comfort and checking my injuries. He kindly bandaged me with torn bits of his own clothing. With an enormous effort, he managed to lift me onto his own donkey and took me to safety. He paid an innkeeper to care for me and promised to come back and pay more if needed. Such overwhelming, undeserved, humbling kindness.

GET ACTIVE

Have an acts of kindness day. Think of lots of ways to show kindness to others and to yourself. This could be simple things like smiling at people, right through to doing someone's gardening for them or offering to make a meal. Look out for little ways to show kindness, and see how it makes you feel.

Maybe you could have an AoK (Acts of Kindness) day once a month or even once a week.

TAKE NOTICE

Write yourself a letter as if it is from God to you. Take a look at Psalm 139 or Psalm 23 if you aren't sure what God might be thinking of you. Take time to write true things like the fact that God loves you, that he will never leave you, that he has good plans for you (Heb. 13:5; Jer. 29:11). Send the letter to yourself and read it slowly once a week.

GIVE

A question to chat about

What is the kindest thing someone has done for you this week, or that you have done for someone else?

An idea to try

Start an AoK day at your school or in your circle of friends, when you try to do as many kind things in a day as you can. Look out for all the kind things done to you too.

A blessing of kindness

God, you are so kind
Please fill my heart and mind
so I can show real kindness too
and my kind acts will point to YOU

L is for Lament

CONNECT

Lament is a funny word, and not one we use very often. In fact, when I was younger I don't think I had ever heard this word. It is all about how to express sadness and emotions when you aren't feeling good, so I wish I had known about it, as keeping all my sad feelings down made me feel quite ill.

The psalms in the Bible are full of lament. The psalmist who wrote these fantastic poems and songs was really good at expressing how he felt when it wasn't positive. There is even a book in the Bible called Lamentations that is full of what we might call moaning and complaining. I didn't use to think it was OK for Christians to complain to God at all. So, when I wasn't feeling happy and thankful, I just stopped talking to God and thought he might have left me.

Of course, God never leaves us, so learning to lament was a big part of my recovery. I learned to write prayers and poems that some people might have thought were a bit rude to God. I was letting out all my feelings, not just the pretty ones.

I love that my granddaughter is being taught that it is OK to cry when you are sad. Her parents just say that she is having a lot of big emotions; they don't judge the emotions by saying things I used to say to myself, like 'Cheer up' or 'Turn that frown upside down' or 'Don't be so grumpy', or even worse, 'Don't be a cry-baby'.

Have people said things like this to you, and does it make you hide how you feel?

It is OK not to be OK and talk to God about all of it. He cares and he knows you.

LEARN

It's OK to cry JOHN 11:1-46

It must be OK to cry; Jesus did it. As you read this, have a think about why Jesus cried. He knew things would turn out OK.

Martha and Mary were worried. Their brother, Lazarus, was so sick, every breath a struggle, he no longer ate or even tried to speak. Jesus would help. They sent messengers to ask him to come.

Time was ticking and Jesus still hadn't arrived. Martha and Mary were concerned. Maybe the message hadn't got through. Maybe he didn't realise how serious the situation was.

Then Lazarus died. They lovingly wrapped their brother in grave clothes, wiping away the tears so they could see what they were doing. Friends had come from nearby towns to grieve with them. Together they placed Lazarus in a tomb, a cave with a stone for a door. Then Martha, Mary and their friends gathered to remember. For four days they told stories of Lazarus' life.

A friend arrived at the house to say that Jesus was just a few minutes away. Martha, always ready to act, left immediately to meet him. Mary went later. Both said the same thing to Jesus. 'Lord, if you had been here, my brother would not have died' (vv. 21,32).

Jesus saw their tears, their pain and their disappointment.

'Jesus cried' (v. 35).

Then he asked to go to the tomb. The crowds of mourners followed expecting Jesus to say a comforting prayer, a few stories of happy times with Lazarus.

'Move the stone away,' Jesus said (v. 39).

The people glanced at each other, checking they'd heard correctly. Jesus must have known that this wasn't right.

Martha turned to Jesus and spoke up. 'But, Lord, it has been four days since he died. There will be a bad smell' (v. 39).

A couple of friends looked to Martha and Mary, who nodded to confirm that they should do what Jesus asked them. Reluctantly they gripped the large rock and heaved it to one side. Everyone seemed to shrink back. But Jesus still stood, calmly facing the tomb. He called out a special prayer for Mary, Martha and all their friends to hear.

'Father, I thank you that you heard me. I know that you always hear me. But I said these things because of the people here around me. I want them to believe that you sent me' (vv. 41–42).

Then he shouted, 'Lazarus, come out!' (v. 43).

After a breathless pause, the impossible became possible. There was something almost comical when poor Lazarus tried to walk, pulling the grave clothes loose. Jesus had to prompt the awestruck watchers to help him. Martha and Mary found the shift from mourning to rejoicing a little overwhelming. Jesus still had the tears in his eyes.

Death doesn't have the last word when Jesus is around, but it's still OK to cry.

🏃 GET ACTIVE

Try writing a sad song or poem. If you don't know where to begin, just start with how you really feel. You can end your song or poem with something you know is good and true about God, but you don't have to if you aren't feeling like it that day. Not all the psalms in the Bible end with praise to God, even though a lot of them do. It seems it is OK not to be OK with God too.

Try making a bit of music to go with your words. Use the minor notes, the sad-sounding ones.

Have a good cry if you need to. Find a friend or someone to listen to why you are sad.

📝 TAKE NOTICE

When I feel a bit low, I like to do a thing I call bubble and soak. I pick a piece of music and I put my headphones on and find a cosy place to sit. I then wrap up in a blanket and listen to the whole song with my eyes shut and picture God holding me tight, whatever I am feeling. I have a few favourite sad songs, often ones without words, classical music, that helps calm me. When the song is finished, sometimes I read my own lament to God, and then I feel better for doing it and letting it out. Sometimes I need a real hug from a friend or family member too. It is OK to ask.

🤲 GIVE

A question to chat about

What helps you express your sad and negative emotions?

An idea to try

In a little group, share ideas for music and poems that can help when you are feeling different emotions, and have a listen to each other's songs and poems. Maybe make a little book and collect some Bible verses that help too.

A blessing for your lament

Whatever you are feeling
Super-happy
or so sad
Know that Jesus knows you best,
Knows every feeling that you've had
So tell him what is on your mind
Worry, sadness, fear
Whatever you are feeling
May you know that he is near

M is for Meditation

CONNECT

One of the things that really helps my wellbeing is meditation. This is not the same as just reading words or thinking about them. For me, it is a bit like breathing in and breathing out words that help settle me down and make me peaceful.

I always choose a short phrase from the Psalms, because I know God is in these words and believe them to be full of God's strength.

So, every day I sit with my cuppa and put my feet flat on the floor, knowing God has put me on the earth right here for this day. The chair I sit in holds my weight, and I think that it is like God holding me up. Then I choose to breathe a few deep breaths and remind myself what the phrase is that week. I change the phrase each week so I don't get bored, but some people just have one phrase like 'God loves me' or 'Loved, loved just as I am' or simply, 'Peace, love and joy today'.

I sometimes set a timer for a minute or two so I don't keep having to check and see if I've done enough. It sounds weird, but it is really hard to choose what to fill your mind with and to sit quietly. It is easy for my head to start running off and thinking about 100 other things. But I find it really settles me to have a meditation phrase and then, a few times a day, to pause and breathe and remember what is true, and fill my head with that.

I attach meditating to my drinking a cup of something, mostly because I do like a cuppa. So every time I take a drink, I remember to do the meditation. You might have a water bottle that you drink from during the day that could be your reminder to have a little pause. It is amazing to me that I can choose what to think about, as I spent so many years worrying about everything. That is like meditating, to be honest, as it is going over and over something.

I found worrying didn't help my wellbeing, but meditation on God's Word does.

 **LEARN**

The Lord's Prayer LUKE 11:1-4

How good are you at concentrating? If you are like me, you might find it difficult to focus on one thing. When I'm praying, I get easily distracted. I think this must have been a problem for one of the disciples. In this story he asks Jesus for help with his prayer times.

I asked Jesus a question today. Ever felt like your question is one that everyone else might think is stupid? I felt like that. Perhaps the other disciples had already got the hang of prayer. I mean, it's about the most important part of being a disciple. But my prayers were jumbled and often ended with me wondering what was for tea. I would sometimes list all the things I needed, or all the people who were poorly or sad. I

would sometimes suggest to God some good ideas that I felt he should take on – things like getting rid of our enemies, or giving us a cure for leprosy. I liked to watch Jesus pray. Sometimes his lips would move but I couldn't hear his words. Sometimes he'd use his whole body to pray, kneeling, or opening out his arms like a massive hug for his heavenly Father. And sometimes he prayed for us, with us – opening our eyes to the kind of conversation that is possible with the Creator of the universe.

I spoke up, looking only at Jesus and avoiding any judgemental expressions on my friends' faces. 'Lord, teach us how to pray . . .' (v. 1).

Jesus gave us a simple and beautiful answer. As I reflect on my Lord's Prayer, I'm so thankful that I asked. He has opened my eyes to so many important things.

He began with the word 'Father' – I almost wanted to ask if he meant it. I understand that he is God's Son, but that we get to speak with such familiarity is ridiculous. For me, it will take some getting used to.

He showed us that even God's name is holy and our greatest desire needs to be that God rules on earth like he does in heaven. When I think about that, my mind explodes. I find it impossible to imagine Love ruling on earth – and yet I am willing to pray for it, to dream about it.

Jesus then showed us what we really need from God – our daily bread and our sins forgiven. He added a little phrase that made me wince. This forgiveness comes as we forgive others. I might need to do a bit of work on that.

Temptation was his next focus. He's already taught us that when we want to do something we know is wrong we should meditate on what God has said in his Word. This was a reminder of how important it is that when we are tempted to do wrong, we make sure God helps us to do right.

Here's the prayer as Jesus said it:

> Father, we pray that your name will always be kept holy.
> We pray that your kingdom will come.
> Give us the food we need for each day.
> Forgive us the sins we have done, because we forgive every person who
> has done wrong to us.
> And do not cause us to be tested.

vv. 1–4

I am so thankful for his simple phrases. All plain enough for me to understand. I still sometimes let my thoughts be ruled by my rumbling tummy, but Jesus has felt hunger too; he understands.

GET ACTIVE

Pick a meditation phrase. Maybe choose something from your favourite psalm or Bible verse, or a short phrase about how God loves you and cares for you.

Now try saying this over and over in your head in time with something like bouncing a ball or skipping. I sometimes do this when I am walking the dog in time with my footsteps.

Make a poster of your meditation phrase and stick it next to your bed.

TAKE NOTICE

I like to keep a journal. This is just a nice notebook that I write my prayers and thoughts in, or do some drawings.

At the top of the page each day I carefully write my meditation phrase. Sometimes I write it several times in different colour pens or different styles. It helps me remember it. I sometimes do a little drawing to go with it.

GIVE

A question to chat about

What meditation phrase would you choose that is good and true?

An idea to try

How about starting a little meditation group? I used to invite a few friends round for a cuppa and then we would set a timer and do a few quiet minutes together. Shared silence is weird at first, but it can be a lovely way to practise meditating. If just sitting still is too weird, you could try it with bouncing a ball against a wall or hopping whilst saying a meditation phrase.

A blessing for meditation

May your quiet moments
be filled with his Word
May your head be clear of worries
so the truth can be heard

N is for Names

CONNECT

Do you like your name? We didn't choose our names, did we? They were chosen for us. It has taken me a few years to like mine. I used to wish I was called Aimee, not Ruth. Don't know why! I just liked it better.

Sometimes people call us names too, which stick in our heads. Sometimes they are nice pet names that people we love call us, and sometimes they are mean.

I really like that the Bible says God calls us by name, that he knows our names and even that he has our names inscribed on the palms of his hands. I'm not sure what that means except that God really, really likes my name and me.

I also like to think every day of God's name. He is called by loads of names in the Bible. 'Prince of Peace' (Isa. 9:6) is my favourite and also 'good shepherd' (John 10:11). Each day I pray online with folk from our charity, and the first thing we do is say as many names of God as we can think of to help remind each other who it is that we are praying to, and to thank him for being all the things his name says he is.

Names are important.

In our Renew Wellbeing spaces, one of our big principles is 'Names not labels'. We don't need to know everything about someone when we first meet them, like what is wrong with them, so we can fix it. No, we just need to know that person's name and try to remember it for next time we see them, so that they feel loved and welcomed.

He knows your name.

LEARN

Zacchaeus come down LUKE 19:1-10

Did you know that Jesus sometimes changed people's names? When he first met Peter the disciple, he was called Simon, which means 'hearing', but Jesus changed it to Peter, which means 'Rock' – then he said, 'I will build my church on this rock' (Matt. 16:18). In this story, Zacchaeus didn't need to change his name, he just needed to change his lifestyle to match it!

In Jericho, when you heard the name 'Zacchaeus', it caused a groan.

'That lying, double-crossing tax collector doubled my tax last week. We all know why. I reckon only a quarter of that goes to our occupying armies, our enemies. As for the rest of it, that dirty cheat keeps it. I don't

know what I hate more – the Romans using it to conquer more countries, or Zacchaeus using it to furnish his fancy house.'

From his name, it seems to me that Zacchaeus' parents had different plans for their son. His education gave him the advantage over others in Jericho, but made him a target for the Romans. They looked for anyone greedy enough to turn against their own people and yet intelligent enough to keep lists and totals. But his parents looked down at their newborn tiny infant and saw his purity. 'Let's call him Zacchaeus. Pure. That's a lovely name.'

How ironic. With impure motives and dirty schemes, this little man made himself rich and extremely unpopular.

Then Jesus came to Jericho. It was soon clear to Zacchaeus that standing with everyone else would be pointless. He wasn't quite tall enough to even see between the forest of heads. As an intelligent man, Zacchaeus knew it was no good asking folk to let him stand at the front. He would have to think outside the box. The only place he could think of was where a sycamore tree spread its branches over the road.

It turned out to be a genius idea. He even found a thick enough branch to sit on that might not be described as comfortable, but it was secure. What a great view. In fact, this branch meant that Jesus would pass directly beneath – except he didn't. He stopped. 'Zacchaeus, hurry and come down! I must stay at your house today' (v. 5).

Zacchaeus nearly fell off his branch. Did he hear that correctly? Did Jesus know his name? Had people been gossiping? Perhaps they'd told Jesus that he'd stolen their money and used it to buy all the pretty things that lined his rooms. As Zacchaeus tumbled out of the tree, thoughts were tumbling through his head. He realised that having Jesus in his home would be a huge honour, and yet at the same time, this man was pure and good and seemed to know him.

He could hear the grumbles around him; it was clear that Jesus choosing Zacchaeus was an unpopular choice. Zacchaeus didn't want Jesus to be criticised. In his heart he knew having Jesus choose him meant a need for a fresh start – he wanted to be pure.

In a loud voice, Zacchaeus spoke to Jesus but hoped the crowds were listening too. 'I will give half of my money to the poor. If I have cheated anyone, I will pay that person back four times more!' (v. 8).

What a transformation. Jesus was telling the crowds how salvation had come to Zacchaeus. It's not that surprising, really. Just being in the presence of God's Son made people want to be pure. Jesus was given his name for a reason too – Jesus means 'God saves'.

GET ACTIVE

Have you ever seen those name plates or signs that some people have on their desk at work or on their office door? I used to wonder whether it was in case they forgot who they were! I think it is more to help other people know who they are.

So how about making a name plate or sign for your door or desk, or both? You can use paper, card or even wood, and draw or paint with whatever you have to hand. You can make a sign using technology if you have access to a printer.

Use your favourite fonts and colours.

Celebrate who you are.

TAKE NOTICE

Play the alphabet game in your prayers today. Try to go through the alphabet praying for people you know whose names begin with each letter of the alphabet. There may be a few you can't do, like X.

GIVE

A question to chat about

Do you like / dislike your name . . . and why?

An idea to try

See if you can remember the names of everyone in a room full of people you know, like your class or church. Find out any names of people you didn't know, and see if you can remember them next time you see that person.

One lady said she liked coming to our Renew space because 'Now someone knows my name'. She said she could go all week and not hear anyone say her name. It made her feel very lonely.

Names are important.

A blessing for your name

Jesus, name above all names
Thanks that you know my name too
and that every person that I see
is known and loved by you

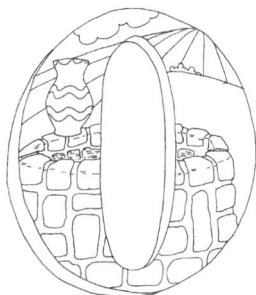

is for One

CONNECT

We often talk in Renew Wellbeing about the economy of one. One seems like a very small number, doesn't it? We usually want more than one thing, more than one friend, one biscuit, one pound. We are often taught that more is better, but Jesus teaches me that just *one* person is worth so much. He went out of his way to spend time with one person at a time. He treated every one person he met as special. He called people one at a time.

He owned nothing and said we didn't need to own loads of stuff. I wonder sometimes if having lots of things and lots of people around us means we stop being thankful for the one thing or one person.

It is amazing to me that when Jesus came to earth to give his life to make us free, that he would have done that just for me . . . just for the one.

I often try to work out if something is worth my time or effort by numbers, but Jesus has an economy of one.

We try to practise that in our Renew spaces by saying that the team would turn up and feel it was worthwhile doing a Renew space for just one person. It is not about numbers.

More isn't always better; sometimes one is enough.

LEARN

Well well well JOHN 4:4-42

Whilst the Bible does have numbers in it and talks about crowds of people coming to Jesus, we also get lots of stories of Jesus spending time helping and transforming the lives of individuals. I wonder if his disciples thought he was wasting his time with individuals? Here is one example.

We'd left Jesus sitting by a well; he'd been really, really busy and deserved a break. The twelve of us set off to the local town for food. One person mentioned that we might have left Jesus by a well, but it was the middle of the day, the hottest time, and he didn't have a single means of getting the water out of the well.

We needn't have worried. When we came back with enough packed lunches for thirteen of us, Jesus was drinking from a cup given to him by a woman. This might not seem strange to you, but we live in a culture where men don't talk to strange women, and they certainly don't talk to strange Samaritan women, never mind ask them for help!

They'd had a long chat and he'd mentioned that he could offer her 'living water' (v. 10), the type that meant you never got thirsty again. This led on to him explaining that he'd come from God and was the one everyone had been waiting for.

Whilst we worried about Jesus' reputation and about the time wasted talking to one person when there were towns full of people who needed his help, Jesus seemed content that he was exactly where he needed to be, and this one woman was worth his time.

Well, she was impressed and rushed off to get her Samaritan friends. Seeing the crowds of Samaritans approaching was a bit alarming, and we urged Jesus to come away and eat some of the lunch we'd brought. He basically told us he didn't need food just then. He said his food was to do God's will (v. 34). He wanted to focus on one thing. One person. A Samaritan woman who needed his help.

Jesus started talking about how the fields were ready to be harvested, we just needed to look. I think now he meant that he could see that this one woman was ready to accept that he was God's Son, the Messiah. Sharing time and truth with this one lady could have eternal consequences.

And it did. Not just for this lady, but for lots of Samaritans that came because she shared her story.

And now as I think about it, I'm so glad Jesus spends time with me. He called me, he knows my name, he helps me wher I am confused; he cares about me. Jesus has compassion on crowds, but he lovingly transforms us one person at a time.

GET ACTIVE

Why not have a big tidy up of your things? Decide what things are really important to you, and give away those things you don't need anymore. You may come across one thing that is really precious but has got lost among all your other things. Give that object a good place to live and be looked at. Choose one item to give as a special gift to someone you know would appreciate it. Ask first before you start giving stuff away, please.

TAKE NOTICE

As you pray today, ask God to show you one thing to be thankful for, one thing to pray for and one thing to say sorry for. I find praying 'the ones' – one thank you, one please, one sorry prayer – can help me take notice of what God is saying and doing that day.

GIVE

A question to chat about

What one thing is really, really important to you?

- -

An idea to try

Try picking just one habit that will help your wellbeing every day – like the cup habit, an exercise, a prayer, or an AoK – and making it your one thing.

- -

A blessing for the one

Help me to love you, Lord
with all my heart and soul
Make all the broken bits of me
into one loved and loving whole

P is for Present

CONNECT

I love the letter P. In my alphabet of wellbeing, this is the letter I can think of most words for. Prayer, partners, peace, pace, play . . . all wellbeing words for me. Maybe you could write your own alphabet of wellbeing top tips. I wonder what you would pick for P? I have chosen the word 'present'. This is not just because I love presents, and I do. I love giving them and getting them! But this word 'present' also means being right here, right now, with your attention fully in this moment. The Hebrew word in the Bible for presence means turning to face someone. I like that. I spend quite a lot of time with my body being present somewhere, but my head being somewhere else. (Well, not my whole head! That would be weird. I mean my thoughts.)

Sometimes I take the dog for a walk by a lovely canal with beautiful trees and birds, and yet when I get back home I realise I didn't really see any of them because I spent the whole walk thinking about, or worrying about, something that I was going to do and say that day. I am learning to try to be present in the moment God gave us.

That is why it's called the present. It is a gift from God.

LEARN

Peter's past problems and future fears MATTHEW 14:22-36

Are you a worrier? Do you think about the past and the future more than the present moment? Here's a story where Peter the disciple really needed to focus on the moment he was in and who he was with.

Having just waited on thousands of people while Jesus fed them all with a tiny packed lunch, Jesus offered to send the crowds away so we could hop into our boat and sail over to the other side. We didn't need asking twice. We didn't stop to notice the gathering clouds.

From the boat, we could see all the crowds wandering off and Jesus heading up a mountainside to pray; we watched him until he was a tiny dot, too difficult to make out.

That's when the wind picked up. Increasingly threatening waves started to batter our boat. By the middle of the night, with no light except the houses on the distant shore, we were really starting to worry. One of the waves started to look too tall and thin . . . then with eyes straining, we could see it wasn't a wave at all, it was a person, in the middle of the water. Now the waves weren't the problem. What was this freaky vision in front of us? A ghost?

'Have courage! It is I! Don't be afraid' (v. 27). It was Jesus' voice. I don't believe I really thought before I spoke, it just seemed like something I didn't want to miss out on: 'Lord, if that is really you, then tell me to come to you on the water' (v. 28) I shouted over the wind.

Jesus told me to come. This was it, my moment. With a bit of difficulty, I swung my legs over the side, and stretched down with my right foot. I felt my sandal hit a solid surface! My eyes like saucers looking at Jesus as he smiled back at me, I lowered my other foot onto solid water. I must have taken quite a few steps, revelling in this astonishing moment, slap bang in the middle of a Jesus miracle, my eyes fixed on his chuckling face and my legs stepping forward, one faith-filled stride at a time. 20 seconds of complete trust, the best 20 seconds of my life.

And then I over-thought it.

I remembered the disciples behind me, the fear we had of the growing waves. I thought about how this might end. I was standing on water; it couldn't be done. What was I thinking? My past problems and my future fears filled my head and I decided to look around and assess my situation. Yes, I was right; the waves were too big, the boat was too far away . . . I was going to drown.

The water crept up my legs, grabbing at my clothes and pulling me down. I couldn't remember what direction Jesus was in. So I yelled, 'Lord save me!' (v. 30).

He was there, lifting me and safely guiding me back to the boat. Again, I was focused on Jesus, back in the present moment and sure of his protection. As soon as we got into the boat, the wind stopped. And in that present moment Jesus was in charge – one eyebrow raised at my doubts. A holy, silent second in time.

GET ACTIVE

I like to play a presence game sometimes. Knowing that God is always present to us, I set a timer to ping every hour on my phone. (Only do this if you aren't with other people that it will annoy!) When it pings, I stop for one whole minute if I can, and just try to notice my breathing, what is around me, the sounds and smells I may have missed, and the fact that God is with me, all around me and within me. Then I thank him and carry on with what I was doing.

TAKE NOTICE

There are two things I have tried that help me to be more present to the God who is present to me. One is called zoom out, zoom in. I stand outside and zoom out, looking at the sky or something massive and really seeing it. Then I zoom in on something really small, like a flower or an ant or my fingerprint, and thank God for the details.

The other thing I do is when I am eating something, I sometimes try to see how long I can make it last. This can work with a grape, or a sweet, or a raisin; just taking time and really noticing the taste and texture of the thing and being thankful for it, rather than gulping something down. This can help us to be more present too.

GIVE

A question to chat about

Do you find it easy to be really present when you are with other people, and really listen to them? What helps you do this?

An idea to try

Try taking turns with your friends, and talk for a whole minute each about something you are interested in without anyone else interrupting. Then wait a moment or two to think about what has been said before asking any questions. Take turns to speak and listen, and see if this helps you be present to each other, rather than thinking about your own stuff when someone is talking to you.

A blessing to be present

God of the past and the future
I choose to be present today
Help me to be fully here and receive
the gift of your presence, I pray

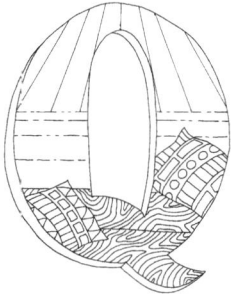

Q is for Quiet

CONNECT

I am not a naturally quiet person. Are you? Some people are. I have had to learn about how important quietness is to my wellbeing. When I wasn't well, I lost my voice for nearly a year. At first it was funny, then it was worrying and eventually it was really annoying. I could not join in conversations. I could not sing, or shout, or laugh out loud. I started to feel I was not even really me anymore. It got lonely.

I did learn to sign a bit and used little cards that I would write things on that I wanted. But I was so very, very glad when I got my voice back, and now I try to look after it a bit better, and have voice rests when my throat gets sore or I have been talking a lot.

One of the things we did when I was still a teacher and my voice was bad, was that every hour we would take a voice break together in class.

Everyone would take a book to read or write in, and I would play some music and we would all lie or sit on the carpet and take a 5-minute break.

The children loved it, I loved it and I don't think we learned any less. In fact, because there was time to think a bit, I think we all learned more. Sadly, when I felt better, we stopped doing voice break time, and it all got noisy again. We stopped practising being quiet, and it does take practise.

There is a verse in the Bible about God 'quieting' us with his love (Zeph. 3:17, NKJV). Isn't that lovely? A God who quiets us.

LEARN

Peace and quiet MARK 4:35–41

What do you like to do after a busy day? Curl up on the sofa? In this story Jesus chooses a cushion in a boat to rest on, a little sanctuary of quiet.

Jesus had been talking all day to crowds of really interested people. They sat quietly on the ground and listened to Jesus calling out great stories about seeds and lamps and helping everyone to understand God better. After a particularly busy day of teaching, Jesus suggested to his disciples that they all got into a boat and crossed to the other side of the Sea of Galilee. It's more of a massive lake, about eight miles wide.

Jesus found a cushion and made sure he wasn't in the way, whilst his friends, some of whom used to sail on this water a lot when they were fishermen, took charge of the boat. In the peace and quiet of the boat, with the hushed chatter of his considerate friends and the slapping sound of the little waves, Jesus soon drifted off into a peaceful sleep, a deep and wholesome sleep that helped his body to prepare for the next

crowd of eager listeners . . . So deep that he didn't hear the disciples and the weather as both gradually got a lot louder.

'Peter, look at those black clouds, they're getting closer pretty quickly,' said John in a hushed voice so as not to wake Jesus.

A few minutes later, Peter's voice had to compete with the whistling winds as he called out, 'James, bring down the sail quickly, the wind is getting too strong!'

Again, a little later, now yelling at the top of his voice, John tried to compete with the howling winds and crashing waves: 'Fasten down everything that's loose!'

The non-sailors were clinging to the sides of the boat, drenched as angry waves smashed over them. Turned out where Jesus was, just under the bow, the front of the boat, was the best place, protected from the waves. But surely he couldn't still be sleeping in this storm?

'It's too much for this boat John,' bellowed Peter. 'I can't see the land, and we're in danger of capsizing. Time to pray.'

'Or rouse the man himself,' suggested John. In his loudest voice he shouted, 'Someone wake Jesus!'

'Teacher! Do you care about us? We will drown!' (v. 38).

Jesus opened his eyes, saw what he'd been missing, stood up and told the storm off. 'Quiet! Be still!' (v. 39), he called out with authority. Then he sat back on his cushion as the black clouds disintegrated and the huge waves meekly flattened into submission. The only sound was that of the panting disciples, still catching their breath from the storm and now glancing at each other with wide eyes.

No one dared to speak. It was eerily quiet, especially after the racket that the storm was making and the high-pitched panicky screams of the disciples.

Eventually Jesus, looking at their faces, broke the silence. 'Why are you afraid? Do you still have no faith?' (v. 40). They weren't sure if he was talking about their fear of the waves or their new fear – a fear of Jesus!

One of them leaned over to John and whispered quietly, 'What kind of man is this? Even the wind and the waves obey him!' (v. 41).

GET ACTIVE

Make a fabulous den and call it your quiet space. You can make dens indoors or outdoors. I love to use bedsheets and pegs to make great dens. You can make a den almost anywhere: under a table, in a little corner, behind the sofa.

Put up a 'Shhh' sign so people know the den is your quiet space, and spend a bit of time just being quiet in there each day. Make it cosy and comfy with some cushions and a good book or a notebook and pens. Enjoy.

TAKE NOTICE

Invite a friend or two to try out your quiet space. It can be really hard to do quietness together, but it is lovely when you decide to give it a try and you don't feel the need to speak all the time. God loves to share quiet moments with us.

GIVE

A question to chat about

Do you find quietness calming or scary? Why?

An idea to try

Use the timers you made in an earlier activity, or make some if you haven't already done this, to time how long you can be quiet for especially with your friends and family. Make a game out of it.

A blessing of quiet

Help me be calm enough to hear
that you don't need all my busyness
and words
Quiet me with your love
God who is near

R is for Renew

CONNECT

This is one of my favourite wellbeing words. You might have guessed that, as I named a whole charity Renew Wellbeing. I really love the idea that God is making all things new. He takes what is old and broken and makes it brand new by forgiving us and breathing life in us.

The habits in this book help me to be renewed in my head too. My thoughts and feelings can also be made new when I choose not to discard them or ignore them, but instead let God have them all and see what he can make with all the broken pieces of my worries and fears.

I love it when instead of throwing something away it can be upcycled or recycled into something new.

We do lots of upcycling in our Renew centres. Old jumpers become bags. Old furniture gets sanded down and painted. Old newspapers and

magazines become jewellery and decoration for boxes. Old bits of wood get made into spoons. Old shirts get made into bunting. It is fantastic to see what can be done with things that could be thrown away.

God is always making us new and never throws us away because we get a bit broken.

LEARN

Being made new JOHN 3:1-21

The Bible talks a lot about being made new. 'I will put a new way to think inside you' (Ezek. 36:26). Here is a story about Jesus talking with a clever man about being completely renewed. The clever man doesn't really understand. Do you?

Nicodemus was an important person in Jerusalem. He had been studying the old part of the Bible (because this was before the New Testament existed) for a long time. And when the Jews wanted to know something about their religion they went to Nicodemus. He'd read in his Bible that God was going to make everything new and that he would send a rescuer, a Messiah. He wanted to know if he was on the right track, if he was part of God's people. Nicodemus was really interested in Jesus. He was doing some amazing miracles and teaching people some radical things about God that made even the clever people want to know more.

He went to find Jesus at night. I'm not sure whether it was because Jesus was very busy in the daytime, or because Nicodemus knew that the other religious leaders, the Pharisees, would be angry at him for meeting with this man who was causing trouble. Most Pharisees really didn't like Jesus.

'OK, Jesus,' Nicodemus began. 'I've seen and heard what you can do, and I've decided you must be from God.'

Jesus smiled and then threw in a statement, seemingly from nowhere, that made Nicodemus hold his breath. 'I tell you the truth. Unless you are born again, you cannot be in God's kingdom' (v. 3). How did Jesus know Nicodemus had come to ask about being part of God's people? And what on earth was he talking about? Getting back in the womb and being born again? That couldn't be right, thought Nicodemus!

But Jesus knew what Nicodemus needed. He needed a fresh start. He needed to understand that just learning more or trying to be good wasn't what God wanted. God wanted to renew people – forgive all their sins, wipe out all their mistakes, change their motives and ambitions, reset their thoughts about others, inspire their actions to be completely loving, set them on a new path. Basically, Nicodemus needed to know that he had to be born again, not just add a bit to the life he already had.

Just as it is impossible to be physically born again, it is impossible for people to be renewed by themselves. We are always making big mistakes, being selfish, upsetting God. But with Jesus now on earth, God had put into place his plan to make everything new.

Jesus helped Nicodemus to understand God's plan.

'For God loved the world so much that he gave his only Son. God gave his Son so that whoever believes in him may not be lost, but have eternal life' (v. 16).

Believing in Jesus was the key to this teaching. God's kingdom, his new heaven and new earth was for everyone who had come to Jesus to be made new.

GET ACTIVE

It is time to get upcycling. Have a look round the house for something that is being thrown away – an old cardboard box, a jumper, some wrapping paper. It could be anything. If there really isn't anything, try a charity shop and see if there is something made of wood you could sand down and repaint.

Take a good look at the old item and see if you can make it into something new and useable: pen pots, storage boxes, little gifts for others.

Enjoy making things new.

TAKE NOTICE

The Bible talks about God 'renewing [our] minds' (Rom. 12:2, NIV). As you pray today, picture your mind and your life like a clay pot that God is making and carefully moulding into shape and filling with his love.

GIVE

A question to chat about

Have you ever upcycled anything? What did you make?

An idea to try

In our Renew spaces, we sometimes make an agreement with a local charity shop that anything that needs repairing we will repair or renew, and then give it back to them to make more money for charity. Maybe you could join a Renew space doing this, or ask your church to start one. You could just do this as a group of friends.

A blessing for renewing

God, take all the scattered pieces
of this broken place we live
And carefully mosaic us
into a new creation
Designed to love and give

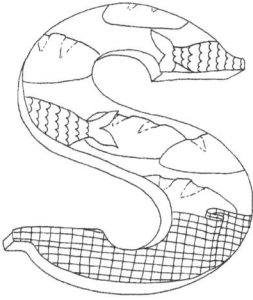

S is for Simple

CONNECT

This is another of my favourite words. It didn't used to be. I grew up in a time when people who were unkind called other people simple, and it wasn't meant as a compliment. Now I see that to be simple is a really great thing for my wellbeing. Keeping things simple, leading a simple life, enjoying simple things: these are things I now actively try to do.

Just because something is simple does not mean it is easy. There are very successful businesses that have learned how to make just one or two things really, really well rather than make loads of stuff quite well. I am learning to keep it simple in my life by working out, with God, what he made me to be. There are no two people the same on the planet. You are uniquely you. And I am uniquely me. There are some things that we can all do and be, like being kind and sharing, and being loving and forgiving. But there are some things that I just don't need to do or be.

I am writing this book with my lovely little sister, Debbie, because she is great at drawing and storytelling. God doesn't expect us to be able to do everything by ourselves. He made us with special gifts, skills and characteristics that make us great at some things but not everything.

It helps my wellbeing when I work out what to say yes to and what is someone else's thing to do and be.

LEARN

A simple choice JOHN 6:1-15

Do we make things too complicated? When we are hungry, we need to eat. When someone else needs something, we need to share. When Jesus speaks, we need to obey. Simple. The little boy in this story simply chooses to do what is best.

Crowds wandered past our house, following the teacher, Jesus. 'Mum, I'm going to walk round the lake,' I shouted.

'What! Now? It's nearly lunchtime. There's some bread and fish on the table, take some of that,' she called from out in the backyard.

Not wanting to miss anything, I grabbed everything off the table and ran out of the house.

I ran through the chatting groups of people and got myself right to the front. I sat with Jesus' friend Andrew. People were still gathering when I heard Jesus mention bread. One of his other friends, Philip, told Jesus they couldn't afford to feed the crowd and that it would take a year's wages.

I tugged at Andrew's sleeve. 'Excuse me, I have more than I need. I'm happy to share mine if you're hungry.' I'd realised whilst running round

the lake that perhaps Mum had meant me to take one barley loaf and one fish, but without thinking I'd cleared the table and shoved it all in the nearest bag.

'Well, that's very kind, but I don't think you'd have enough for this crowd. How much do you have?' Andrew replied, smiling kindly.

I looked for the first time to discover I had taken five loaves, as well as two fish. Andrew turned to Jesus. 'Here is a boy with five loaves of barley bread and two little fish. But that is not enough for so many people' (v. 9).

At first, I nearly contradicted Andrew. I was actually only offering to share with him. I hadn't offered it all. But then Jesus caught my eye and he looked excited. He was about to do something remarkable and I didn't want to miss out. It was a simple decision to make – ask to keep part of my lunch or give it all to Jesus and see what he would do with it. He knew something I didn't and I couldn't wait to see what it was.

Jesus asked the disciples to help him get everyone to sit down on the grass in groups. Then he took my hessian bag, gave thanks to God, pulled out each loaf and broke it up, placing the pieces into large baskets so the disciples could give it out. Bread and fish kept flowing; more and more of my mum's delicious freshly baked barley loaves came from Jesus' hands in big chunks with big pieces of fish, enough to make a nice sandwich. Andrew handed me some quite early on and it was delicious. I don't remember it ever being so filling. Andrew told me that there were 5,000 men in the crowd, so if we add in all the women and children, my packed lunch had just fed a ridiculous number of people. And he said they collected twelve baskets full of leftovers. I couldn't wait to tell Mum.

I had made three simple choices that day and I was so glad. I chose to follow Jesus, I chose to share my lunch and I chose to say yes to Jesus. Best decisions ever.

GET ACTIVE

Make a 'simply me' poster for your wall. On the poster you can draw or write the things that make you uniquely you, and any special Bible verses or stories that speak to you. Keep having a look at the poster when your head gets a bit full and you get a bit busy, and see if you are maybe doing or being something that is someone else's thing to do or be.

Just be you.

Make the poster with all your favourite colours and pictures. Keep it simple, with not too many words, so you can remember to keep decluttering your head.

TAKE NOTICE

Ask God to show you a simple verse or phrase that becomes your 'simply me' words. For our charity Renew Wellbeing we have three little phrases:

Be present

Be prayerful

Be in partnership

These three little reminders help us to keep what we teach churches and do in our centres very simple. You will know how easy it is to let your room get messy and how hard it is to keep it tidy. It can be the same with our minds. A simple phrase or a few words that describe what God has made you to be can help you decide how to live, and what decisions to make.

GIVE

A question to chat about

What habits or words do you have that help you keep things *simple*?

An idea to try

Have a big tidy-up in your room or one of your drawers. Get everything out and lay it all out so you can look at each thing and decide whether you need to keep it and if so, where should it live. Make some boxes with labels to help keep everything organised. (I am not good at this, by the way, so I am telling myself to have a go too!)

A blessing of simplicity

May the God who simply loves you
help you to live a simple way
May you know exactly who you are
and choose life with him today

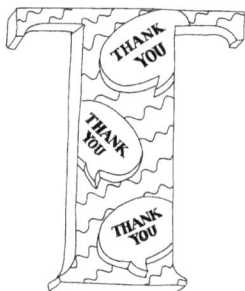

T is for Thanks

CONNECT

It is great when someone thanks you for something, isn't it? When I was a little girl, my mum used to make us write thank you letters to all our relatives to thank them for Christmas presents, straight after Christmas. I remember feeling like it was a bit of a chore and complaining, but it took very little time and I know that the people who got the letters were so happy to receive them. It isn't that we give things expecting to be thanked. But it is lovely to know how a gift made someone feel. Now it is even easier because we can send a quick text message to someone.

But because being thankful felt like a chore, I haven't always worked out how to be honest and thankful in my chats with God. My prayers used to be more like a shopping list where I asked God for loads of things, and quite often I forgot to thank him for anything.

These days as a charity we start each day thinking of all the things we want to thank God for, and then we chat to him about the things we need, and say sorry for what we got wrong. Starting with thanks has been really helpful for me, as I can forget to see the good things when there are things that need God's help.

Can you imagine what God must feel like if we keep on asking and never thanking him when he has made the whole world and then come and saved us too?

Even on days when I am feeling low and need to be honest with God and have a moan, there are usually one or two things I can spot that make me thankful.

Don't worry if there are days when you can't be thankful. It is OK not to be OK.

LEARN

Heartfelt thanks LUKE 17:11-19

It takes a little extra effort to say thank you. Are you an 'extra effort' type of person? This story from the Bible about ten men with leprosy is a perfect example of this.

We'd been sent out of the town to live in our unhealthy huddle. Ten of us tried to help each other; all of us had leprosy. Our families sent food out and left it at a special place, but it wasn't the same. We might see them in the distance and wave a thank you, but our skin disease meant we needed to stay far away from everyone who was healthy.

One day we found out Jesus was travelling from Galilee to Samaria, so we had a pretty good idea which road he'd be on. When we spotted him in the distance, we were so excited.

'Jesus! Master! Please help us!' called out one of my friends (v. 13).

'Go and show yourselves to the priests,' Jesus called back (v. 14).

We all looked at each other. We knew what this meant. When people, and this was rare, got better from leprosy, the first thing they had to do was show themselves to a priest. The priest would check them over and when it was felt safe, they would be allowed back to normal life, back to family.

We all turned and started walking, then running towards the town. As we ran, we felt life and wholeness flooding into our bodies. I glanced at my hands; all the sores had gone and there instead was skin like the skin of a teenager – not just healed but better than ever. I stopped. 'Guys! We need to thank him!' But they ran on, too excited to pay attention. I stood for a moment, deciding whether to stick with my friends. No, I had been brought up to say please and thank you and I'd never been more thankful in my life.

With energy like I'd never known, I raced back to the road where we'd seen Jesus. 'Praise God! Praise God!' I was yelling as I arrived. I threw myself down at Jesus' feet, 'Thank you Jesus, thank you. You have changed my life. Praise God for sending you. Thank you.'

'Ten men were healed; where are the other nine?' he asked (v. 17).

I looked up into his face, raising my eyebrows as an answer. 'Is this Samaritan the only one who came back to thank God?' I resisted the urge to tell him that I had suggested we all came back. 'Stand up and go on your way,' he said. 'You were healed because you believed' (vv. 18–19).

We had all believed, we were all healed, but only I got to be face to face with the most remarkable man that's ever lived. It was worth the extra effort to see him and thank him. Now I had to visit the priest, and then I could look forward to hugging my family.

GET ACTIVE

This week send some thank-you messages to a few people. It might be a thank you for being a good friend, or a thank you for a gift you received. It could just be a 'thank you for being you' message. Why not make a few thank-you cards ready to send in the post too. It is still lovely to get a letter or card, so if you make some colourful thank-you cards now, you will always have one ready to pop in the post when the time comes to say thank you to someone. You don't even have to post them; you might be able to pop it through their door or leave it where they will find it.

TAKE NOTICE

Sit quietly and try to think of something to be thankful for beginning with every letter of the alphabet. It gets harder when you get to the end of the alphabet, of course, so you can miss some letters out!

GIVE

A question to chat about

What are you thankful for today, right now?

An idea to try

Play the thank you alphabet game with some friends or in a group. Maybe make a set of cards to go with it, or make it into a board game. Being thankful can be fun.

A blessing of thanks

Thank you, Lord
Just thank you loads
For friends, for breath
For frogs and toads
For a tiny flower and a massive tree
And thank you, Lord
For making me, me

U is for Unite

CONNECT

I wonder if you support a football team? If you do, is it one of the ones that has the word 'united' in it? Sorry if it isn't and that question made you mad!

The reason teams use the word 'united' is that it is such a strong word to suggest that these players will be able to work really well together, that they have one purpose.

That is why I think it is a good word for my wellbeing. We don't do so well on our own, and lots of people get very lonely. But just because you have people around you doesn't always mean you are united.

The word 'unite' means all the parts or people coming together with a shared interest, purpose or goal. I have seen this happen in our Renew spaces when different churches in a town all work together to open a café space. In one of our centres, every church put some money in the pot and then they were able to have a café on the high street open all week. Isn't that great! One church couldn't have done this by themselves but together, united, they could do amazing things.

As a mum I love it when my children help each other and play nicely. I think God feels like that about us.

Jesus told us that he came so that we could be one, united, with one love, one goal, one purpose (John 17:22).

LEARN

Like little children MARK 9:33-37

How are you at seeing good in other people? Do you find it easier to notice the annoying things they do? Which do you think Jesus prefers? In this story, Jesus' disciples got it wrong, and Jesus needed to help them understand the importance of unity.

Being a disciple of Jesus has been really interesting. Twelve of us spending every day together. I've been wondering today why Jesus chose us. I suppose we have things in common: all Jewish, all men, all young; but apart from that, so much that divides us. A tax collector and some fishermen, brothers Jesus nicknamed 'sons of thunder' (I will leave it to you to imagine why) and some who speak first and then think later, some without much education, and some without any! A jumbled bunch of confused sheep. So many times we've had to ask Jesus to explain what he's been teaching us, and then so many times when we haven't asked because we've been too embarrassed to admit we don't understand.

If I had chosen disciples, I think I'd have chosen two well-educated older men who weren't so opinionated and annoying. We argued today. I can't even remember how it started, but it ended up being an argument about which one of us was the greatest. We were walking to Capernaum and just out of earshot of Jesus, but he could tell there were raised voices. There are some real hot-heads in our grumpy group.

Once we reached the house in Capernaum, Jesus asked us what we were arguing about on the road. It suddenly dawned on me that we should be ashamed of ourselves. No one spoke. We all realised that Jesus had spent all this time teaching us about loving and serving, about sacrifice and unity, and we had been yelling over each other, listing each other's faults and trying to shout about all our achievements. Not our finest moment.

Even though we didn't answer, he knew. He said, 'If anyone wants to be the most important, then he must be last of all and servant of all.'

A toddler holding a little wooden boat had been leaning on Jesus' knee, smiling up into his face. Jesus lifted him into his arms and we all melted as the child giggled and stroked Jesus' beard. He talked about accepting children and how much it pleases him. And that when we are kind and put little children first, it's as though we are accepting him, which in turn makes God happy.

Each of us had lowered our heads; we gave each other sideways sorry glances. Arguing about who was the greatest was obviously something Jesus really didn't want us to do. He wanted the opposite. He wanted us to put those who seem small and unimportant first. He wanted us to serve and help those who can't help themselves and he wanted us to be a team – working together, seeing the good in each other, being loving and humble. It seemed obvious as we looked at this toddler and the way he and Jesus were playing together. The child was giggling and shrieking with delight as Jesus 'accidentally' knocked the little toy boat off his knee and acted surprised. Over and over he does the same thing, knowing this game brings a beautiful belly laugh that fills the room and makes us all smile. What a delight there is in putting someone else first. Looking round at my friends, I noticed something else that united us – we were all belly-laughing at the game Jesus played, all of us like little children.

GET ACTIVE

To help me understand how important it is for me to be united in my own head, to make room for all my feelings and let them work together, I sometimes think of my life like a cappuccino, a hot drink with coffee, milk and chocolate. It needs all the ingredients united together. Why not invent your own hot or cold drink that needs at least three ingredients to be really tasty? Plan it out first on paper and write a recipe. Then ask if you can try making it. You may need to try several different combinations to get the right mix.

TAKE NOTICE

Invite some friends round to taste the drinks and maybe have some snacks. Everyone could bring something to share. As you share food and drink, imagine Jesus sitting with you and enjoying you all being united.

GIVE

A question to chat about

Talk about a time when you felt really united either with other people, with God, or just within your own head.

An idea to try

Join a team, or get some friends together and make up a team game. See how well you can work together.

A blessing for unity

Just as you are three in one
Unite us all in love
Like the Father
Spirit
Son

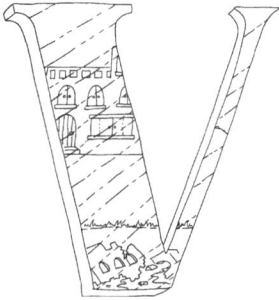

V is for Values

CONNECT

Our values are sometimes hidden and not something we even think about. But we all have values. If you value friendship, you will look for and be a good friend. If you value fun, you will make sure you play lots. If you value honesty, you won't be able to settle until you have said sorry when you haven't been completely truthful. If you value generosity, you will be someone who loves giving gifts. If you value health, you will eat well and exercise often.

Our values at Renew Wellbeing are around our three phrases:

Be present
Be prayerful
Be in partnership

This means we value quiet spaces and encourage people to take time to pray. It means we like to show up and sit down and do hobbies together, rather than trying to fix each other. It means we want to know people's names, not their labels, and like to ask for help when we need it and offer help when we can.

Working out what our values are can be tricky, but I have found it really helps my wellbeing to know them, so that when I feel out of sorts, I can ask God to show me where I have not stuck to my values, or where I am valuing something that isn't good for me. The great thing is that God always forgives us when we ask him to.

His values are love and forgiveness, and he values us.

LEARN

Built to Last LUKE 6:46-49

Have you ever made a mess because you thought you knew best? Ever ignored an instruction manual and regretted it? I have. God's values are the best ones to build on. Jesus tells a great story to help us picture this.

Jesus told us a story of two builders. The first one, we'll call him Victor, knows all about the best way to build and he realises that if his house is going to last, he needs to dig down deep until he's found a solid foundation. The second builder, we'll call him Vinnie, knows all about the best way to build as well. He sees Victor digging and decides that no one will see what's at the bottom of his house, so Vinnie just finds a flat bit of sand and starts to put up walls.

Both houses look the same. And whilst the sun is shining, both houses are great places to be. But the sunshine can't last forever. There are always going to be storms. Storms bringing wind and rain, puddles and problems. Victor's house with the solid foundation is fine. Inside Victor enjoys peace and safety. He might prefer the sunshine, but he knows his house will last through the storm, and that by obeying the rules of building he can be sure of the outcome – his house won't budge.

The storm is a much bigger problem for Vinnie. Same wind, same rain, but these puddles are starting to wash away the sand below his walls; big cracks start to appear, and eventually a whole section of the wall comes crashing down. This wall was holding up the roof and it isn't safe for Vinnie to even stay in his house. Vinnie stands outside, the wind messing up his hair and the rain dripping off his nose. He feels hopeless.

Jesus used this story to explain how important it is to actually do what he says. Crowds of people spent time hearing what Jesus had to say. But only some of them would put it into practice.

GET ACTIVE

One of the things that I have to help me remember my values is a little book of important words that sits by my desk. It is a nice blank sketch book, actually, with lovely crisp white pages. If something feels important to me, I turn a page and pick a really great pen, and write the words in big bold letters. I sometimes draw a picture to go with the words. I have some Bible verses, some promises from God, some things that people have said about me that are encouraging, and some other bits and bobs. For example, one page says 'Simple, joyful, gentle' because I love these three words. Another page has the verse in the Bible that says that God will never leave us (Heb. 13:5). Another page says, 'Be still' in big letters (Ps. 46:10).

I look at the book and add things to it most weeks. It helps me remember my values.

If you are part of a group reading this, you could make a big 'values' banner for your group.

TAKE NOTICE

One thing that helps my values is to read a little bit of a Gospel every day so I get to see Jesus' values. I want to be more like him, so reading a little bit of Matthew, Mark, Luke or John each day helps. I want his values to become my values.

GIVE

A question to chat about

What do you think your values are, and how can you see what you value in the way you behave?

An idea to try

Take a look at the Five Ways to Wellbeing. Connect, Learn, get Active, take Notice, Give . . . we call it Clanging. See if you can make clanging into a way of being today. Could the Five Ways to Wellbeing be used as values?

A blessing for your values

May the God who values you so much
show you what is great
May you be someone who brings God's love,
a really brilliant mate

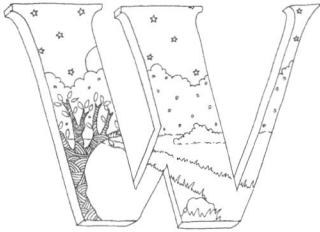

W is for Wait

CONNECT

I'm not very good at waiting for things. So, putting the word 'wait' in my alphabet seems a bit odd. How can it be good for my wellbeing to do something that I am not good at? Well, I have discovered that while I am waiting for something or someone, I can be learning a lot about God's peace and patience. When I wasn't well, I just had to wait to be better. Whilst I was waiting, God taught me how to wait more peacefully, rather than getting frustrated and angry. Some of the habits I still have today I learned when I was waiting.

So, the habit of deep breathing and using psalm words to calm my mind in meditation was learned whilst waiting to feel well enough to get up and about. Learning to do a hobby and be really present was all learned during waiting times. So, waiting can be an active thing.

There are several words in Hebrew (the language the psalms were written in) for waiting, and one of them is *Qavah*, which is the same word used of a spider spinning a web. The spider is waiting to catch a fly for its breakfast, but it waits actively by making a web.

The things I learned in my waiting helped me catch God's goodness and notice God's peace more. It is like a web of wellbeing.

LEARN

Waiting well MATTHEW 26:36–56

Sometimes we wait well, and sometimes we don't. In this story, Jesus knows what's coming and uses his waiting time really well. The disciples don't.

In many ways, Jesus has been waiting for this moment since he was born. He came to be our sacrifice; he came to take our punishment. After thirty-three years of waiting, there was only one more night and Jesus, knowing what was best, took his disciples to an olive tree garden to pray.

It was night time, a strange time to go to a garden. Peter, James and John could see that Jesus was troubled. 'Sit here while I go over there and pray,' Jesus told them (v. 36). He explained that his heart was full of sorrow, that he needed to pray and that they should too.

Jesus knew that to be strong enough to go through with the plan meant staying close to God. The disciples waited, but also found comfy places on the ground and allowed their eyes to close.

Jesus prayed for an hour, asking God to show him if there was another way, but he also made it clear that he wanted to do what was best. He wanted to rescue people from sin. After an hour, he found his disciples had fallen asleep whilst waiting. He knew that the next few days were going to be terrible for them too; they would need God's help.

'Stay awake and pray for strength,' he said. 'Your spirit wants to do what is right. But your body is weak' (v. 41).

Jesus went away and prayed again. 'I pray that what you want will be done,' he said (v. 42).

When he checked on his waiting friends, they were asleep again.

Jesus prayed a third time, saying the same thing. But this time as he went back to his three sleepy friends he could hear the sound of a crowd approaching through the trees. No more waiting.

'The time has come,' he said (v. 45). All of a sudden Judas, the disciple who'd turned against him, was there with a crowd of people carrying swords and wooden clubs, all sent by the religious leaders who hated Jesus.

The disciples weren't ready, but Jesus was. He quietly went with them whilst the disciples all ran away and left him. They would have to wait a few more days to see God's plan. Three days of waiting, three days of feeling lost, frightened and alone.

But then the wait was over. Jesus stood among them and showed them how God had beaten death. Another short wait and then God would send his Spirit to live in them and always be with them.

GET ACTIVE

Take a look at some spider's webs. Try to see if you can watch a spider making a web. It is amazing.

Maybe you could try to actually weave a web yourself using string or thread. It is quite tricky. Spiders are very clever.

TAKE NOTICE

Choose the longest queue you can when paying for something in a shop or waiting in line. Whilst you wait, notice how it makes you feel and talk to God about it. Pray for the other people in the line.

GIVE

A question to chat about

How do you feel about waiting, and what is the longest time you have had to wait for something?

An idea to try

As a group, have a go at waiting, and try different ways to make the waiting time more peaceful.

A blessing for waiting

*May you know that the God
who waits for you
waits with you
And will give you patience
as you wait for him too*

X

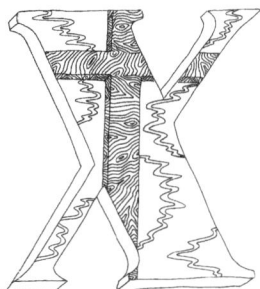

Marks the Spot

CONNECT

I bet you have been wondering what on earth I could choose as a wellbeing word beginning with X! Could X-rays or xylophones be good for my wellbeing? Well, it won't surprise you to know that I have cheated. You might have to too, as you make up your wellbeing alphabets. X in my alphabet marks the spot on a treasure map. When I was a teacher, my favourite activity was making massive papier mâché islands, and hiding treasure on them. I can't remember what I was trying to teach, but it was fun. When the treasure was hidden, we would make maps to remind ourselves where the treasure was, and mark the spot with an X like the pirate maps I had seen in films and books.

So, what has that got to do with wellbeing? The thing is, I have noticed times and places in my life that have been like treasure to me. There are times or places where God has spoken to me or where I have felt lots of peace. Some of these places are easy to keep going back to, like my special chair where I do my morning prayers. Other places are further away and I don't get to visit often, like Ffald-Y Brenin retreat centre in Wales. Some places always feel like treasured places; for example, being by the sea. Some treasure spots are moments in the past when I feel like I came across God and some truth about wellbeing. Each of these places I mark with an X by jotting them down in a journal or notebook. The journal then becomes my treasure map so I can remember all the wonderful things God has shown me about his peace.

I wonder what places or times are like treasure for you?

An even more amazing thing about treasure is that we are 'chosen', special (1 Pet. 2:9). So we are God's treasure! He gave up everything for us. I find that incredible.

An X marks my life and your life as God's treasure.

LEARN

At the cross MARK 15:37-39

A moment of realisation. One second where treasure is found. X marks the spot. This is a story of one Roman soldier stood at the cross, not an X on a page, but a cruel, tall, wooden cross with Jesus on it.

I'd heard all the rumours, I'd even caught a glimpse of the man before, which was usually difficult with the crowds around him. They said he could make fish suddenly appear; this was after fishing boats had unsuccessfully been out all night. Sounds fishy to me all right. Stories of paralysed people suddenly jumping to their feet. But was he really paralysed? This man has a thing about water, it seems – turning it into wine, walking on it and making huge waves of water into instantly flat calmness! Then those reports we got that a 12-year-old girl and a bloke

called Lazarus had been raised from the dead! After the first few stories I put it down to a publicity stunt, but as more reports came from different people of new and impossible events, I started to wonder. There had to be an explanation.

Then there was his teaching, the other thing he was famous for. I've heard the Pharisees with their lists of rules, but this man taught something different. He told really memorable stories – one about a coin getting lost and the joy of finding it, one about houses built on different foundations and the importance of good solid values to build your life on. He told farming stories about seeds and surprising stories about selfish priests and helpful Samaritans.

So, I've watched this man with interest since his arrest. He has stayed calm and humble the whole time. He's not blamed anyone or shouted, he hasn't changed his story or pleaded for his life. He seems to have the most amazing self-control.

He never does anything selfish; he speaks to common criminals like they are important to him. He patiently endures the evil mocking and the crown of thorns. His face, although so injured, radiates light and his eyes look on others with love. Even me. Not only is this man innocent, he's absolutely perfect. The Pharisees have got it so wrong. They've taken the man they've waited generations for, their Messiah, and tried to get rid of him.

There are other rumours I've heard. Rumours that this man Jesus said he would rise to life again. Anything is possible. He can still storms, heal wounds, transform matter – he can do it.

It's over, and as I've stood in silence here at the cross, I feel like I've just witnessed the one who invented life facing death. The longer I watched him, the more I became convinced that this man isn't from this world. 'This man really was the Son of God!' (v. 39).

GET ACTIVE

Make a treasure map of your life, and mark on it all the times and places where you have learned something about wellbeing and God's peace. Maybe you could make it into a big island with craft materials or construction blocks. It could be fun to mark all those spots with an X and see if you can remember what each X was about next time you look at the map or model. You can make a game out of this with some friends too.

TAKE NOTICE

Use a notebook or journal to draw or write down any times or places of wellbeing, or where God has been close to you. You can jot things down every day, every week or just every now and then. Thank God for each moment. If you have a special prayer place, go there often.

GIVE

A question to chat about

What places are special for you? How do you feel about being God's treasure?

An idea to try

In a group, make one big treasure map and mark on it all the special places and times when each of you has learned something good about wellbeing with different coloured Xs. Take turns to pick an X and talk about what treasure is buried there.

A blessing for treasure

Right here in the present my treasure lies
God, you are my treasure
You are my prize
And wonder of wonders
as I follow the clues
I am finding that I am
your treasure too

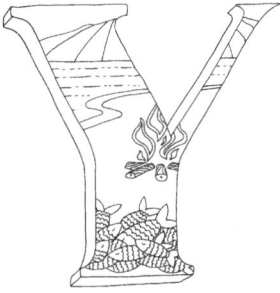

Y is for You

CONNECT

As we come towards the end of the alphabet, it now gets personal because Y is for *you*. Yes, you are really important to God. You are loved. You are special. You are unique. You are made to be you on purpose by God. I have been learning this for years, but I still sometimes struggle to believe I am loved just as I am. I often try to be more like someone else that I think God is more pleased with. I often wish things about me were different. It is taking a long time for me to really accept myself. This is odd too, because I have a very loving family so I'm not sure where I picked up all these lies about not being good enough. It must be even harder for those of you who haven't had kind people around you. My heroes are those of you who keep believing in God's love and keep being yourselves even when life has been tough. Thank you for teaching me things.

You see, even though this is personal, we all need each other, and our wellbeing affects all those around us. How we treat others can help them know they are important and loved.

When I talked in 'X marks the spot' about you being the treasure and making a map of an imaginary island to show treasure in your life, I realise that we are not islands. I was born and brought up on a little island and sometimes I forgot about the rest of the world, but we are all connected and we all need each other.

You are a gift from God to this planet too. You matter. Just be you. Don't try to be anyone else.

LEARN

Let's talk about you JOHN 21:1-17

Remember Peter's story right back at the beginning – letter A for acceptance? He didn't feel good enough to be with Jesus. In this story he's back feeling that way again. But Jesus has other plans.

Peter was, of course, excited that Jesus was alive again, and he was amazed that Jesus had beaten death, but mostly Peter was feeling guilty. When Jesus was arrested, he ran off. When people pointed Peter out as a disciple, he said he didn't know Jesus – three times! Guilt. It hung around Peter like a heavy cloak, making him feel like he wasn't good enough for anything. He couldn't look anyone in the eye, worried that they'd see his selfishness.

He needed a distraction from his gloomy thoughts so he suggested a little fishing trip to his friends.

A whole night and no fish. Now Peter felt guilty and useless.

A man on the shore called out to ask if they'd caught anything. Nope. He shouted a suggestion about using the other side of the boat. Peter

rolled his eyes – yes of course, how simple! All the fish were just hiding on the right, and they'd only looked on the left . . .

But the nets, now lowered over the right side of the boat, filled with fish and John looked at Peter with a grin. 'It's the Lord!'

Peter didn't think twice, he jumped in the water and swam to Jesus. It was the third time Jesus had appeared since his resurrection, and Peter didn't want to miss it.

They had a lovely breakfast on the beach and then Jesus turned to Peter. 'Let's talk about you.' Peter didn't look up, didn't look Jesus in the eye. He still felt guilty.

Three times Jesus asked Peter if he loved him. Three times! Did Jesus know that three times Peter had said he didn't know him, when he was arrested? Peter expected he did. Jesus told Peter he had important work for him to do, taking care of the sheep and lambs. Not actual sheep and lambs – Jesus was describing the new Christians that needed help.

Peter remembered Jesus asking him to fish for people three years before, just after another miraculous catch of fish, and now he needed to shepherd them. Now he could look Jesus in the eye. And in Jesus' eyes he saw acceptance and love; he saw that Jesus had big plans for him and when he focused his gaze, he saw a reflection of himself. He was Peter, the rock, accepted and loved.

GET ACTIVE

Make a list of the things that make you unique; add in a few pictures, draw some of the things you are good at. The alphabet in this book started with accepting yourself, so you could try saying something nice and kind to yourself every time you look in the mirror.

TAKE NOTICE

I know that sometimes we can get it very wrong and make big mistakes. Sometimes it is hard to admit we have made a mess and still accept ourselves. Take notice of where you are finding it hard to forgive yourself.

One of the things I do every day is use the prayers at the end of this book to help me keep on being forgiven. It is like having a reset or turning a fresh page. It is so wonderful that God loves and accepts us as we are but also wants to make us clean and more like Jesus every day.

Forgiveness helps us be more ourselves, and then we can forgive others too and help them be more themselves.

GIVE

A question to chat about

What makes you, you? What are you good at? What do you struggle with?

An idea to try

How about thinking of something encouraging to say to everyone you meet today and then actually saying it?

A blessing for you

> You
> are Unique
> There aren't
> two
> like you
> It's amazing that God loves me
> and sets me free
> and that
> you are the only you
> and I am the only me

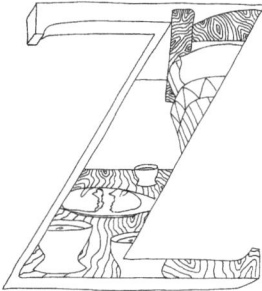

Z is for Zzz

So we arrive at the end of our alphabet of wellbeing with another tricky letter. I would love you to have a go at writing your own alphabet of wellbeing – writing things that help you find peace and God's love. What might you choose for this letter? Maybe zoos or zebras help you? Maybe you love a zip wire . . . they can be fun and therefore good for your wellbeing. I couldn't think of anything clever so I just wrote some zs and it looked like I was snoring. Zzz.

That made me realise how important good sleep is for my wellbeing, and how badly I sleep when I am worried about something. It also made me realise that this alphabet thing is never done. When we get to the end we start again, just like when we go to bed and go to sleep, we wake up and get another day to have wellbeing adventures.

This then got me thinking that it is OK not to be OK some days, because that day will close and a new one will open and God will still love me.

It helps me to realise that we can get things wrong sometimes and start again. We can have a bad day and turn the page for a new day.

Going to sleep and waking again is the best rhythm I know for wellbeing.

It is a brand-new start every day.

I wonder what helps you get to sleep. I have a few top tips from lots of years of not sleeping well and being a worrier. I will share them later in the chapter.

For now, isn't it good to know the Bible says God doesn't sleep (Ps. 121)? He watches over us and never leaves us.

So, we can sleep soundly, knowing he will still be with us when we wake up.

 **LEARN**

Like a dream LUKE 24:13-35

Imagine waking up to a day that feels hopeless, and then miraculously everything changes and it becomes the best day ever. This story follows two disciples who'd given up hope. They get the new beginning, the brand-new day feeling.

It had been such a terrible few days in Jerusalem. Cleopas and the other disciple were chatting about what they'd seen and heard. Jesus' arrest at night in the garden, the trial where people told lies about Jesus, the soldiers who had treated him so badly. They tearfully recounted all they'd seen at the cross, the nails, the crown of thorns, the death of the one who had brought life and joy. They talked about their shattered hopes and dreams. They'd thought Jesus had been sent by God to rescue them, but now that was all impossible. Then there were the

rumours that the tomb was empty. But the women who said that simply couldn't have got the right place.

There was nothing to stay in Jerusalem for now. Best get home to Emmaus and enjoy their own comfy beds after what should have been a Passover party in Jerusalem and turned out to be their worst nightmare.

Another traveller walked at their pace and asked what they were chatting about. Both disciples looked at each other, puzzled. How had this man not heard? It was the only thing being talked about in Jerusalem. But as they told their sad story, this man seemed keen to help them understand something. He started talking about Moses, a man they knew lots about from their Scriptures. Every old story he told from the Scriptures helped to explain the big plan God had, a plan that included Jesus coming, his death and resurrection. The stories were about sacrifice and love, about forgiveness and rescue. The two disciples were gripped by every word. What amazing insight this man had – he seemed to make everything relevant and alive.

It was getting late as they approached their home in Emmaus. Time for something to eat and comfy beds. They persuaded their new friend to stay.

As this man picked up the bread and broke it and gave thanks to God for it, the two disciples suddenly saw who he was. It was Jesus! They looked at each other open-mouthed. In that second, Jesus vanished.

No longer sleepy, the two disciples jumped up from the table. 'Let's go and tell the others.'

The seven-mile walk – which was more of a skip, really – back to Jerusalem seemed so short as they excitedly went over all that Jesus had explained to them on the road. Each time Jesus had showed them something new they were overwhelmed with joy, as though their hearts had been burning within them. Their minds filled with new wonders from God's Word.

The rumours were all true. Some of the other disciples had seen Jesus too. Cleopas thought back to his restless sleep the night before; a night filled with hopelessness and worry, despair and emptiness. But tonight, he looked forward to dreaming of the risen Saviour. He could dream about a world where forgiveness and acceptance were possible. Jesus offered a new life with God. Cleopas knew there'd still be problems, but now he also knew Jesus walked with him and could fill his mind with the wonders in his Word.

🕺🎵 GET ACTIVE

People used to tell me that counting sheep would help me sleep. I'm not even sure what that meant. I think I was supposed to see sheep in my imagination and count them. It never worked for me.

There are lots of things that help us, like listening to quiet music, or a story, or playing the sounds of the sea. But I wonder if the sheep thing might be good too. How about taking a look at Psalm 23, which is all about sheep and a good Shepherd, with lots of helpful truth in there to make us feel settled?

Why not make a sheep mobile to hang above your head as you sleep, with some of the key words and phrases from Psalm 23 written on each sheep? Or even make some little fluffy sheep with calming words on them, and keep one under your pillow each night.

It can really help to go over and over something good and true as you go to sleep.

📝 TAKE NOTICE

One of the prayers at the end of this book is an end of day prayer. This prayer has been practised for centuries and is sometimes called the 'Prayer of Examen'. That sounds scary, like an exam, but it's not. It is lovely and peaceful.

Examen or end of day prayer is a way to go back over the day in your head as you close your eyes and try to spot all the things to be thankful for; all the times when you have seen God's love and beauty. It is a bit like counting sheep!

You can also notice all the things that weren't good and say sorry and let them go. I also then notice one or two things I have learned that day and choose to remember them to take into the next day.

GIVE

A question to chat about

How well do you sleep? What helps you sleep well?

An idea to try

Your alphabet of wellbeing can be a good thing to try and go over in your head if you are having trouble getting to sleep or you wake up worried in the night.

I sometimes say to myself:

Ruth, you are **A**ccepted
Breathe deeply
Be **C**ompassionate
Dwell in God
Empty your troubles
Think of your **F**amily and friends
Know that you are **G**rowing
Have **H**ope in God
Think about your **I**nterests

And what brings you **J**oy
Plan an act of **K**indness
Lament for the sad things today
Meditate on true words
Know that he knows your **N**ame
And that you are the **O**ne he chooses
Be **P**resent
Be **Q**uiet
Be **R**enewed in your mind
Keep it **S**imple
Be **T**hankful
Be **U**nited with others
Keep to your **V**alues
Wait for God
Spot where the **X** is
Know that **Y**ou are his treasure
Now sleep **Z**zz

You see, this alphabet of wellbeing is not just words in a book for us – it is a way of life.

Debbie and I pray it will become that for you, too, as you explore your own wellbeing alphabet or as you use ours.

A blessing for sleep

And so to sleep
knowing God will keep
you
He will hold you
because he knows you
best of all
However big
However small
He loves you
Sees you
Is ever near you
This God of wellbeing
will help you
to be you
So rest, just rest
God knows what's best

Prayers

Some prayers to pray each day[2]
Morning prayer: Psalm 103

Get comfortable in your chair and close your eyes if it helps you to focus. Take some slow deep breaths and relax.

Be still and know that I am God.[3]
Take a moment to pause and be still

Bless you, Lord, bless your holy name.
What do you want to call God today? Friend? Healer? King? Something else?

Bless you, Lord, for all you have given today.
What good things have you got in your life today?

Bless you for forgiving me when I get things wrong.
Think about things you are sorry for today and know that God forgives you.

Bless you for rescuing us from bad situations.
Say the names of places or people that are in trouble and need help.

Bless you that you love me and care for me.
Think about how God loves you and cares for you.

Midday Prayer: The Lord's Prayer[4]

Get comfortable in your chair and close your eyes if it helps you to focus.
Take some slow deep breaths and relax.

Be still and know that I am God.
Take a moment to pause and be still.

Our Father in heaven, honoured be your name.
What can you say about God today?

Your kingdom come, your will be done, on earth as it is in heaven.
Name places around the world that need God's help.

Give us today our daily bread.
Tell God what you need today.

And forgive us our sins as we forgive those who sin against us.
Think about the things you feel sorry for today – God forgives you.

Lead us not into temptation but deliver us from evil.
Tell God about situations, bad things that we need rescuing from.

For yours is the kingdom, the power and the glory, for ever and ever.

End of Day Prayer

Get comfortable in your chair and close your eyes if it helps you to focus.
Take some slow deep breaths and relax.

Be still and know that I am God.
Take a moment to pause and be still.

Think back over your day and notice all the times when you felt God's goodness or been blessed.
What are the things from today you want to say thank you for?
If you would like to, say those out loud.

When you think back, did you notice times when you didn't feel blessed?
When you felt sad, or worried, angry or scared?
If you can, you can leave those situations here.

Who have you met today who needs to have a blessing?
You can say their names out loud if you like.

Finish with the host blessing each person present by name.
(When I led prayers in my adult Renew space I used to say: 'We've come to the end of this Renew time, but as you go, know that you can take this peace and stillness with you.')

Endnotes

[1]Ruth Rice, *A–Z of Wellbeing* (Milton Keynes: Authentic, 2022), p. 77.

[2]We are very grateful to Sarah Fegredo for writing these prayers. See Renew CYF training manual www.renewwellbeing.org.uk (accessed 8 May 2024). Prayers edited for the purposes of this book.

[3]Ps. 46:10.

[4]Matt. 6:9-13. Paraphrased from different translations including NIV, NLV and WEB.

Authentic

We trust you enjoyed reading this book
from Authentic. If you want to be
informed of any new titles from this author
and other releases you can sign up to the
Authentic newsletter by scanning below:

Online:
authenticmedia.co.uk

Follow us:

www.ingramcontent.com/pod-product-compliance
Lightning Source LLC
LaVergne TN
LVHW051119080426
835510LV00018B/2127